STEPPING TO REALITY

BY
James "Chocolate Jimmy" Dockery

Table of Content

About the Author 1

Introduction 2

Chapter 1 3

Chapter 2 7

Chapter 3 12

Chapter 4 19

Chapter 5 28

Chapter 6 33

Chapter 7 42

Chapter 8 46

Chapter 9 50

Chapter 10 54

Chapter 11 60

Chapter 12 66

Chapter 13 70

Chapter 14 76

Chapter 15 79

Chapter 16 84

Chapter 17 86

Final Thoughts 91

References 96

About the Author

James Dockery is a Boston, MA, native who served many sentences in prison due to decisions he made in his life to run the streets. In doing so, he ran into many obstacles, trials, and tribulations, and he suffered from alcohol abuse for many years.

He is now in recovery from his addiction and admits that he is powerless over it. He went through the spin cycle and concluded that the A.A./N.A. program wasn't enough. He had to put in the work and not only learn the twelve steps but also live them. So, he adopted these twelve steps, along with the ten laws of his creator, to work on living a righteous, manageable lifestyle without the burden of a substance.

He lost many loved ones and faced many tough hurdles while fighting to regain his sanity. It took him hitting rock bottom one last time to realize it was time to step into reality.

So, he wrote this book and chose to do his twelve steps with you, the reader, in hopes of being an inspiration for those who think life was meant to be harsh for people who came up like he did. He wants to start his quest to spread wisdom to the youth with the intent of showing them that life is far greater than what was taught. Before any of this is possible, he knows he must give his will and his faith, along with dedication and commitment, to his creator and live by example...ONE DAY AT A TIME.

Introduction

My name is James, and I'm an alcoholic. As I write this intro, I've been in recovery for six months. Within these six months, I have lived a life of peace and gratefulness. Grateful of my creator. For giving me the wisdom and understanding of knowing, with the desire and faith to change, anything is possible. Also, for blessing me with a loving family, and a wife who is going through this journey with me. Lastly, for showing me through trial and tribulations, how to accept things I cannot change, have the courage to change the things I can, and for giving me the wisdom to know the difference.

Now, for the record, I wrote this book three years ago. It took me a long time to move forward with it because during the last few years, I've been living a life of turmoil. So, I told myself, until I find my way back to being a man of positive action, and actually live, what I'm saying in this book, I'm not going to share it and look like a liar.

So, now that I'm mentally in the position I want to be in. I've decided that this is now the time to share my story with you. I've decided to do my twelve steps with you, and the people who took the time to read about my ups and downs, and my ways of learning from them. And how I've came to become the person I am today.

My goal is to reach out to the youth, and to the ones that grew up in a society that was designed for us to fail. No matter what color your skin is or what background you come from. Whether you're rich or poor. We all have our own stories.

I know that it's impossible for me to change everyone who reads this book, but I live by the saying, "If 100 people read my book, but I'm able to change only one… I've done my job. Any more than that is a blessing. You look at yourself in the mirror and can't stand who you see? Hopefully my story and my journey will finally get you to accept, and embrace who you really are, and have the courage to step to your reality, and make a change.

Chapter 1

Step 1: We admitted we were powerless to alcohol – and our lives have become unmanageable

September 27, 1984, I was born in City Hospital in Boston, Massachusetts—home sweet home. My mother, Minnie Reed, better known as Paulette, was a college graduate from Spelman University, top of her class, summa cum laude. She went on to become a medical assistant for people with AIDS. My dad, Willie Dockery, better known on the streets as "Chilly Willy," was a bonafide hustler. Everything he knew was the streets. My grandma, Carrie Brihm, was the staple of my family—the Queen Bee. My big brother, Kenneth Reed, better known as Jay Roc, was a cold gangster. Then there was Uncle Johnny.

You could basically say all the male figures in my family, unfortunately, were negative influences, but none had more of an influence on my life than my Uncle Johnny Brihm. For those who are reading this book and personally know my family and me, if you ask them who I resemble the most, they are going to tell you my uncle. I'm like a melting pot of everyone in my family. I got my good heart and care for other people from the women. I got the hustler mentality from my pops. I got my intelligence and my smart mouth from my mommy, lol. But my personality and my addictive nature, especially when it came to alcohol, came from none other than Uncle Johnny Brihm, also known as Big Brihm. The role my Uncle Brihm played in my life was astronomical. My uncle was an addict. The first time I ever roamed the streets of Boston was with my uncle. My mom used to work from 4:00 p.m. to 12:00 a.m., Monday through Friday. Pops was out hustling, and big bro was doing a bid, so my grandma used to babysit me until mommy came home. I used to love staying at nana's house because that meant I got to hang out with Uncle Johnny. I grew up in the Alice Heyward Housing Development— the Mission Hill Projects. My uncle is what you call a legend in my neighborhood. But when it came to addiction, he lost the war. My uncle died of cirrhosis of the liver.

It's a cold night, and I'm out with my uncle, roaming the streets. It's the end of the month, so he's flat broke. You know, unc used to get his checks on the 1st, so he had spent all of his money, and the 1st wasn't for another week. I said, "Unc, what are we gonna do? You ain't got no money." He says, "Lil nigga, when there's a will, there's a way." He picks up a Pepsi can and says, "See, there's money everywhere." I asked him, "What do you mean, Uncle Johnny?" He says, "Look, I just picked up 5 cents. Every can you pick up is 5 cents apiece. You find 20 of these, it's a dollar." I said, "Uncle Johnny, there are cans everywhere." He said, "Exactly." Mind you…it's cold as a bitch outside! We go from dumpster to dumpster, street to street, picking up every can and bottle we find until we get a whole shopping cart full. My hands are so numb, I'm crying to go home. We finally get to Fuentes Market on Parker Street, count the cans and bottles, and deposit them. It came up to 7 bucks! SMFH! All that walking around in the freezing cold for 7 measly bucks! Mind you, I'm 9 years old. This is my first encounter with what addiction does to you. My uncle and I go to the store, and he buys me a dollar's worth of candy. I thought I came up, lol. At that time, 1 buck would get you a brown paper bag full of candy. Now, at this time, I want you to pay attention because I'm about to reveal the liftoff to my tumultuous history of alcoholism. My uncle goes and buys a 40oz of St. Ides, two nips of gin, Seagram's to be exact (I remember it like it was yesterday, lol), and a half pint of MD 2020. We leave, and my hands and feet are numb. I say, "Uncle Johnny, I can't feel my feet, I'm cold." He twists off the cap of one of the nips and drinks half of it and then says, "Here, lil nigga, drink this." I said, "I'm gonna get in trouble." He says, "If you keep your mouth shut and don't be a lil snitch, nothing will happen." I tip it to my mouth; the gin goes down my throat. It's burning… "Yuck! That was gross!" I start coughing. Unc is sitting there, laughing at me. He does the same to the second nip. "Here." I say, "Uh uh, it's nasty." He says, "Stop being a wuss." I take it and gulp it. OMG! I felt like I wanted to throw up! As we were walking, he's laughing, and I start to feel funny, like a sensation. Then I noticed the inside of my body was getting warmer! I never felt a sensation like this before. If anybody can tell you anything about my uncle, they will tell you Brihm was a funny motherfucker. That night, I realized why. My uncle had a great sense of humor, and with alcohol in his system, my uncle could've been a comedian.

Before we went back to nana's house, we went to the park. I had convinced him that I wasn't cold anymore. As I'm running around, I noticed my uncle kept putting this little white pebble on top of a nip bottle and lighting it. I asked him, "Uncle Johnny, what is that?" He said, "Nothin', but something I better not ever see you doin'." That saying to this day, and that cold stare he gave me while saying it, saved me from ever trying crack cocaine in my life. I had just drank basically a whole nip of gin, so I was running around. Unc says, "Come here, you lil queer (totally disrespectful), take a sip of this beer." Oh yeah… when unc was under the influence, he used to act like he was Dolemite. Everything he said was either a rhyme or riddle. I started to drink the MD 2020. I took a swallow and, to my amazement, it tasted like fruit punch! He gives me another sip, then another, then tells me that's enough. I swear I never felt this good in my life.

That day was the start of my bumpy road of addiction. I didn't go full blast until I was 16. I used to sneak into Uncle Johnny's room and sneak sips of the MD 2020. All the way up to the age where me and my boys would get together every night and hustle up 8 bucks to buy us two 40oz of King Cobra and two Black & Milds. Then, all the way to the first time I got caught smoking weed. My mother would no longer give me money as much as she used to after the fact, which, furthermore, led to me getting my first 8-ball of crack on consignment from my ol' head, all so I could afford to drink and smoke weed when I wanted to.

Now, in the present, as I look back at my life in the past and assess all the times I made stupid choices and did stupid things—all the jail time, the loved ones I've lost, and the friendships that I've severed due to saying or doing things that I can't take back—I've finally accepted that it was all caused by my choice of indulging in alcohol. I am powerless over my disease and not only need help from my creator but also need to help myself by accepting reality. Alcohol, to me, is what kryptonite is to Superman.

Some people say the first step is the most important because, without accepting the fact that you have a problem, you will never be able to fix it. I used to be in denial, blaming my past, family genetics, my addictive nature, or my mental health because I was incarcerated for seven and a half years. It's always easy to blame something or someone else instead of facing reality and accepting that it was your choice to put that bottle to your lips. Yours…and no one else.

Chapter 2

Step 2: Came to believe that a power greater than ourselves can restore us to sanity.

Who is God? What does a higher power or creator mean to you? Throughout my life, I've battled with these questions and must admit I still do at times to this day. I come from a very religious background. My grandmother and my mom were loyal Baptist Christians. They taught me to the best of their ability the ins and outs of Christianity. I'm talking from Sunday school to being in the church choir—you name it, I was a part of it. Although my mom did what she had to do to raise our family after she developed diabetes, she always kept her faith in God.

Now… I say all of that to say this… The last 10 years of my life have made it very hard for me to have faith in a Christian God. At times, I am very angry with my creator (as I would like to call him) for all the bad breaks I caught. Now that I'm older and have the knowledge of knowing my history, I no longer consider myself Christian, but only label myself a child of my creator. For the record, I respect all religions, whether I agree with them or not. I choose to believe there's a higher power greater than me, I just choose not to label. I do believe he gives us the power to create our own destiny; how you choose to live your life dictates the outcome of it.

Throughout this book, I will have flashbacks of moments in my life when I could've made better choices that probably would've ended in different outcomes. Right now, however, I'm going to explain roughly what led me to the decision that it was time to accept reality—that I had a problem I couldn't control.

It's January 3, 2020… the year of the pandemic. The day I was released from a federal correctional institution in Fort Dix, New Jersey. I came home to an apartment that felt empty to me. Normally when I came home from jail, the first thing I saw was my dad sitting on the couch in the living room. The first person I heard was my mom's loud voice. But this time it was different. My nephew Noonies (JayVaughn, but I call him Noonies), my baby nephew Little Rocafella, and my nephew's babymother are there… no pops… no mommy.

I had just finished seven and a half years in the feds. If I told you what for, you would drop your jaws. I want you to feel it, though, so I'm going to tell you: four-tenths of a gram of crack! That's right—less than a half of a gram of crack put me behind bars for damn near a decade. Good ol' Uncle Sam's American justice system. I lost both of my parents while incarcerated. No funeral and no burial. The feds don't allow you to go to your immediate family's funeral. I'm home for the first time in my life without my parents. It led me down a psychological spiral. When I left, my daughter was seven. When I came home, my daughter was 15 years old. My brother's home, but he's an addict running around, terrorizing the streets. To top it off, the room I slept in was my mother's room—same bed, same dresser, same TV. Even my mom's clothes were still in the closet. In jail, I didn't have the opportunity to properly grieve, so when I came home, the shit hit me like a ton of bricks. Mind you… I'm on federal probation and have to wear a GPS monitor on my ankle for a year, all of this… for a forty rock of crack.

I had an overnight job; things were going well. I just couldn't shake the depression, the sweats at night, dreaming my mother and father were still there just to wake up and realize it was just a dream. I said, "Fuck this, I'm not trying to feel this every day." So I started to drown my sorrows with a bottle of alcohol. That choice led me down a road of destruction. The higher my anxiety and depression got, the more I would drink. The more I would drink, I eventually quit my job and continued my dad's business… selling drugs. Mind you, it's the pandemic, I'm on a GPS monitor, in the middle of Nubian Square selling crack, getting drunk all day, and smoking spice.

In my mind at the time, I thought I was the man, and you couldn't tell me nothing. I had the best crack; all the addicts loved me. My girl was fine, and the cops didn't bother because it was the pandemic, and they weren't getting out of the car to risk catching COVID. COVID-19 was a drug dealer's dream… or so I thought. I didn't realize how much my life was headed towards disaster and that alcohol was destroying my body, until one day I'm in the middle of Nubian Station shaking, sweating, getting the chills, trying to figure out what's wrong with me. My boy is like, "Bro… you need a nip." I said, "Fuck nah, you're trippin'." He said, "Watch." The liquor store opens, and he goes and grabs me two nips of E.J. and tells me to drink them. So I oblige and, low and behold, the shakes stop, the sweats go away, and I feel better. I said, "Hell nah, this is bad," but I continued to abuse the Boston. I figured this life was normal and came with drug dealing, so I wasn't doing anything wrong. I was in denial that I had a problem.

I am a reminder to you again… I'm on federal papers, being defiant to my probation officer. I was coming in late, knowing that I have a nine o'clock curfew, and catching dirty drug tests—not because of use, but because of bagging the shit up, not being mindful that the shit goes through your pores (dumbass). I had no cares in the world and was on the brink of destruction. My turning point came when my PO called me one day while I was sitting in the middle of Nubian Square. Mind you, I'm drunk and I'm late for my curfew. She says, "James, where are you?" I snap, "Why are you calling me at 9:30 at fucking night?!" She responds, "Because it's 9:30, and your monitor is indicating that you're not in the house." I bark back, "Why do you call me so much? You act like you're my bitch or something." She says, "Excuse me?" Then she asks, "James, are you okay?" I respond, "Yeah, and I'll be better if you stop calling me all times of the night like you're my bitch." Then I hang up on her.

The next morning, I'm up, hung over. Everyone tells me I was bugging out last night, beating on people and cussing everyone out. I don't remember anything. I get a call… it's my PO. She says, "Good morning."

I say good morning back. She then asks me, "Is there something we need to talk about?" I'm like, "No, why?" She asks, "Do you remember talking to me last night?" I say, "No." She goes on to say, "James, I'm worried about you. You were out past your curfew, you cussed me out for calling you, telling me I'm not your bitch. You don't remember any of that?" I said, "No, Larissa, I don't." She says, "James, I know you're going through a lot right now. Do you have a problem?" I say, "No." She says, "Okay, fine, then I'm violating you," and hangs up.

Damn, now I'm in trouble. WTF should I do? I take a sip of my Hennessy, then all of a sudden, mysteriously, I hear a voice in my head telling me, "Stupid motherfucker, you have a problem, you need help!" In that moment, I realized what I needed to do. I picked up my phone and called my PO back. I say, "Larissa…" She says, "Yes, James." "You are right, I do have a problem." She says, "OK," "What is your problem?" I answer, "I'm drinking too much and losing control." She says, "OK, James, that's what I wanted to hear. Give me a little while, and I'm going to call you back. When I call, answer the phone." I say okay, hang up the phone, and continue on with my day.

Two hours go by. I'm chilling, drinking as usual, enjoying my day. It's two weeks before Christmas. I get the call… "James," I say, "Yes, Larissa." "By one o'clock tomorrow, you are to be at Gosnold Detox Center." I say, "Gosnold? What the hell is that?" She tells me to google it, then call her back.

Now, me being from Boston and coming from a family and a neighborhood that's all too familiar with substance abuse, I pretty much know my fair share of detoxes, but I never heard of Gosnold. So I google it, and what I read and saw almost made me blow a fuse! I call Larissa back and say, "Falmouth, Massachusetts?! Are you nuts?!" She says, "Yep." I say, "Why not Dimock or somewhere closer to my house?" She says it's because she wants me to get proper treatment and not have a chance to run. Now I'm angry! I say to her, "Larissa, I'm not going to Falmouth, you can forget about that." She says, "James, if you're not in

Falmouth at that detox by one o'clock tomorrow, I'm going to have every Marshal in Massachusetts looking for you!" Damn… I say, "OK, I guess I'm going to Falmouth."

Even though we don't always realize it, the creator works in mysterious ways. If I wouldn't have gone through that dilemma with my probation officer and heard that voice which ultimately persuaded me to make probably the best decision I've ever made in my life, I probably would either be dead or hit with a fresh indictment, facing 20 years of my life in prison. What started out being a choice made in order to stay out of trouble ended up being a life-changing experience. I learned later on down the road that my life then was far from normal and out of control. And now in the present, I realize that my creator is with me and not against me.

Chapter 3

Step 3: Made a searching and fearless inventory of ourselves

When you look in the mirror and take a moral inventory of yourself, what do you see? Are you able to look at yourself and feel good about how you've been living so far in your life? Or are you so ashamed of yourself for all the bad things you've said and done towards people that it's hard to look yourself in the eyes? This step was the hardest for me because for a long time, it was difficult for me to look at myself and be honest about who I see. To really take a moral inventory of yourself, first you have to ask yourself a straight-up, honest question: Are you mentally capable of dealing with who you truly are in an unconditional manner? No bias, no struggling with denial? Just straight, flat-out, "this is me." Finally… in my life as I decided to write this book, I was able to sit in my cell one day, alone, and take a real inventory of myself.

I'm going to dissect my character piece by piece: the pros of my character, the cons of it, and furthermore, flashback to the times I've done good deeds and the times I did bad ones. In order to know where you're going, first you have to be real with yourself about who you really are and how you became this person.

First things first, I step in the mirror. I'm looking at myself. The first thought that hits me? "Damn, I'm getting fat!" lol. During my 90-month sentence, I prided myself on how much weight I lost. I came home in good shape. Now I'm looking at myself, and I look like Winnie the fuckin' Pooh. Mind you, I've been chubby all my life, so losing all that weight was big for me. Gaining it back was kind of a disappointment. But one thing I do know is I got a big ass head. The more weight I lose, the bigger my head looks. So being skinny, to me, was a gift and a curse.

Now reality hits… I look at myself. I'm back in prison. WHAT A DUMBASS! I just did all that time and came home doing the same shit.

Doing the same shit like I didn't just go to the feds and spend a third of a decade for a forty rock, playing with my life. The crazy part is I was living pretty good before I got violated. I was in Falmouth, MA, in recovery, working, staying out of trouble, finally living normally. I let temptations of the bottle get the best of me. I recently had just read a book called Rational Steps to Quitting Alcohol by Albert Ellis, PMD, and Emmit Velten, PHD... they call it "Stinking Thinking": the kinds of thoughts, attitudes, and expectations that move us back into substance abuse and out of recovery. Basically, me thinking I got it all figured out. Feeling like I DON'T have a problem. As long as my mental health is stable, I can drink socially. Pure, outright denial! I have a problem. When I drink, I don't have an off button... it's more like off to the races.

Next assessment, my loyalty which is another aspect of my character that is both a gift and a curse. I have a good heart and a willingness to help, but I also have poor judgment about whom to be loyal to. I've been vulnerable to people who take advantage of my good heart, prioritizing those who don't deserve it while pushing away the people who do. I've learned that I've been given a gift: my creator blessed me with the ability to be an orchestrator, a natural leader, and an influential speaker. I've seldom used these gifts to uplift, but instead, I've used them to push negative energy into the world. If I exerted the same energy to be positive, I believe my value to this planet would be more substantial.

Throughout my childhood and most of my adulthood so far, I've been classified as a mediator in most environments I've landed in, whether with my lifelong friends or in prison where politics play a major factor. I don't know whether it's my intelligence or my savviness that elects me for such an assignment. My voice, my logical thinking, the gift of proving I'm right when I'm right—even when I may be wrong—these are all part of it. I ask myself a question: What kind of legacy do I want to leave on this planet when I'm dead and gone? Do I want to be remembered as a positive role model... or a villain? Do I continue to lead in the wrong direction... or change my ways and start to lead righteously? In Falmouth,

I realized that positivity leads to productivity. Negativity leads to two places: either a jail cell or a casket. Either way… you end up in a fuckin' box!

So I'm lying down one night in my bunk, staring at the ceiling, and it hits me. My next observation of who I am and what effect it has on me: For some fucked up reason, whenever I have great things going for me, I go out of my way… to find a way… to throw it all away. It seems like no matter how good I have it, and how fortunate I am, the minute I pick up that bottle and think I've got it all under control, my whole world crumbles, and I eventually hit rock bottom.

It's 1:00 p.m. I'm in front of Gosnold Detox, waiting to be admitted. I'm feeling so embarrassed. All my friends know that I'm basically checking into rehab. I'm from the hood, where the stereotype of detox and treatment is that only drug addicts go to rehab, not people who drink liquor. So I automatically go in with a chip on my shoulder, saying to myself, "I'm nothing like these people, they are drug addicts… I sell drugs, I don't have a problem." Denial.

As a matter of fact, during this 7-day stint, I learned that my addiction is worse. To feed my disease is legal. There are liquor stores, bars, restaurants, and clubs everywhere with an abundance of alcohol. My addiction is the deadliest, only losing to tobacco. But because I come from an environment where drinking alcohol and selling drugs is socially accepted and considered normal—but indulging in heroin and fentanyl isn't—I walked around the detox with arrogance.

Now pausing and coming back to the present for a second, me knowing what I know now about the world of recovery, I know that no one's vices are better or worse than the next. The fight is real against recovering from substance abuse, whichever poison you pick. Also, the government looks at recovery as a big business. Everyone gets a piece of the pie. Your recovery is worth to Uncle Sam as much as your insurance covers. I will explain this in detail later on…

Moving along, at first, I never paid attention in group. For what? I don't relate to these people, so why care, right? Wrong. Actually, not only did I relate, I was a big part of their problem. When I was forced to sit and listen to the testimonies of different addicts talking about the effects of their addictions, the more I listened, the more I felt guilty. It was people like me that fed their problem. I pumped life into their disease, all in the efforts of making a dollar. The stories, the sacrifices, the graphic content of the things these people did to come see people like me for a hit. Abandoning their children to go get high. After the third day, I started to speak and apologize at groups to these people. For the first time in my life, I wanted to change. Then this little old lady came and gave me that opportunity.

It's close to discharge day, and my probation officer hits me right in the nuts with a Louisville slugger. I have to do further inpatient treatment for 90 days at a place called Miller House… O.M.F.G! I didn't expect to stay in Cape Cod for three months. Christmas was five days away, and I thought I would make it home for the holidays, but my PO had other plans. To throw more salt in the wound, everyone else was going to a place called Cataumet, a 28-day treatment center that just so happened to be coed. I'm going to an all-men's inpatient meat factory… Bullshit!

I get a knock at my room door, and it's a recovery assistant. She says, "James, Martha is here to see you." I say, "Who?" "Martha, the director of Miller House." Oh, God! I heard about her all week. From my assumption, I pictured her to be like a drill sergeant. I walk into the community room, and there's this little, short, older white woman standing there. Creator, forgive me, but at first, I'm thinking, "Damn, 20 years ago I would've tried her," lol. We sat down and introduced each other. I could tell by the way she was talking that at first, she was thinking, "OMG, he's a stone-cold crook," but when it was all said and done, to this day, I still look at her as a mother figure. Although, as we speak, she's probably pissed off at me for fucking up.

I get to Miller House. My man Scottie D picks me up from the detox. Scottie is like a mentor to me in a weird way. He's what you call a "white knuckler" in recovery, meaning he doesn't credit NA/AA for his sobriety. He doesn't go to meetings or participate in any recovery at all. He just prides himself on living his best life sober, regardless if he's miserable doing so at times. But he's Ma's right-hand man.

The first observation I catch onto quickly: I'm the only Black person in the entire house! Right away, I said to myself, "Oh, hell nah, I'm not gonna last." I compared myself to being one chocolate jimmy in a bowl of vanilla ice cream. The irony of it is my name is James, so the nickname "Chocolate Jimmy" stuck with me. Throughout my stay at the Miller House, I met some key players that motivated me (and still do to this day) to want more out of life—basically, to think outside of the box. Ronnie C, my recovery coach, was a major inspiration. He related more to me than most because he came from the ghetto like me, been in prison like me, and prevailed. Manny, Buster, Zach, John C, and my main man Nicholas R… all my recovery brothers to this day. My brother Jorge, however, was the one to convince me to give myself a different shot at life and stay in Falmouth.

After 90 days sober, I was feeling and doing phenomenal. I was just waiting on my bed in sober living. Mama Martha introduced me to three individuals who also played a significant role in this chapter of my life: Rick C, Mike B, and J. Cardoza. Rick C was the head of the three; he was Mike B's life coach and J.C.'s sponsor. Martha introduced me to them as a way of connecting me to the town of Falmouth. Besides, they all looked like me… BLACK, lol. The first AA gathering I ever went to was at Rick C's house, but my first actual AA meeting was with my later-to-be house manager and good friend, J. Cardoza. The name of the meeting was "Roots and Causes." There is where I first shared, got my 90-day chip, and realized that one of my biggest vices, if not the biggest, was about to be greatly tested… and that's women.

Women were everywhere, even on Zoom. While I was at Miller House, I had to take a two-week course via Zoom that was a dual diagnosis partial hospitalization program, or PHP. Its purpose was to help maintain your recovery from substance abuse and stabilize your mental health. In this program is where I met the start of my demise, Rebecka G. (Don't worry, I'm going to dedicate a whole section to that story… smh).

But to keep up to par, life was great. I picked up a job doing landscaping with another major figure in my life of sobriety, L. Sylvester. She taught me everything about the trade, from designing a yard to mulching, creating beds, implanting trees, and how to install cobblestones… EVERYTHING. I cherish the moments I had with Lisa because, for the first time in my life, I actually found something I enjoy doing, and furthermore, a skill I can use to start my own business. I got everything I could possibly need in life: a roof over my head, a decent job, and I'm sober. Doors were opening up out of nowhere. Opportunities were coming from every direction. Working with Lisa made me feel like I was an actual Cape Codder. Lisa was there for my rise and was also a firsthand witness to my fall.

It's May, and summertime is upon us. Anyone who's familiar with the Cape will tell you, Cape Cod in the wintertime is boring as hell, especially in recovery. Your days consist of going to work, going to a meeting, then going home, with the occasional going out to eat with fellow recovery members. But NOW THE SUMMERTIME!? Cape Cod is out of this world! The tourists, the beaches, the filthy rich coming to spend the summer in their multimillion-dollar homes, the parties, and, oh my god, the women. It's like you're living in Beverly Hills.

Between the months of May and August, however, is when the most relapses occur. If you can make it past the summer in recovery on the Cape, then you's a bad motherfucker! I guess I'm not, lol, because it led to my downfall. There were certain factors that I believe led to my slip. Not that I'm trying to use them as excuses, because at the end of the day, it was solely my choice to indulge in alcohol. However, these factors assisted my "stinking thinking." First, when I was released from prison in 2020, I came home at the beginning of the pandemic. The world was shut down. I wasn't able to enjoy any of it. Frankly, the only thing to do was sell drugs, eat, drink alcohol, and have sex. Social distancing made it impossible to have a positive social life. Secondly, I never lived in recovery. I never felt I had a problem. I had figured my binge drinking stemmed from my mental health state. Last and most of all… I never dated a rich girl in my life! Which now brings me to the story of Rebecka G.

Chapter 4

In the recovery community, substance abuse and mental health go hand-in-hand. Basically, your substance abuse is caused by some type of mental health disorder. I'm going to use me as an example: My alcohol abuse (according to Gosnold) was caused by my high level of anxiety and post-traumatic stress disorder, better known as PTSD, which was due to my long period of incarceration and the trauma that came with it. Now, although this may be true—my anxiety at times is sky-high (which minority coming from the ghetto isn't?), and yes, my fed bid did numbers on me. Losing my parents, not being able to bury them, and all the traumatic shit that comes with prison, contributed to my PTSD. The big wigs of recovery use mental health as a justification to pump mental health drugs into recovery.

Earlier, I stated that I attended a dual diagnosis partial hospitalization program, also known as PHP. In this program, the psych doctor diagnosed me with anxiety, PTSD, and depression, which led to me being prescribed Zoloft for depression, Abilify for the PTSD, and Clonidine for the anxiety. Pause for a second… Quick moral assessment of myself: I've been taking psych meds like a fucking fiend, or to civilians, an addict. I've just recently discontinued my prescriptions because I realized I didn't need that shit, and I flushed all the meds I have left down the toilet.

I learned what caused my anxiety: overworrying and overthinking. I came up with my own serenity prayer, more down-to-earth and for all walks of life, whether you're religious or not: "STOP WORRYING ABOUT THE THINGS YOU CANNOT CHANGE, FOCUS ON THE THINGS YOU CAN, AND BE SMART ENOUGH TO KNOW THE DIFFERENCE." My remedy for PTSD… Stop festering in the past, focus on now and the future, and stay out of prison. The less you stress and overthink about the things you have no control over, and the more you dedicate yourself to the shit you can, the less anxious and

depressed you will be, and the less dependent you will be on a substance...
POINT BLANK.

Becky, on the other hand, was a different story. I met Becky in the PHP program on Zoom. It was the pandemic, so there were no physical groups, only online. I saw her, and she was drop-dead gorgeous, reminding me of Taylor Swift. My friend requested her on Facebook, and during the two-week period, we texted each other. What I didn't know but was later to find out is that Becky is what you call a "trust fund baby." Basically, Becky is rich, but she also has a mental health illness called bipolar disorder, one of the worst mental health illnesses you can have. Before I continue, I want you to fully understand this disorder so you can really grasp this wild ride I'm about to take you on.

Bipolar disorder is a severe anxiety disorder, or better yet, a major psychiatric disorder. Some of the key symptoms of such disorders are hearing voices, seeing things or people that are not there, believing that people are plotting against you, or believing people can read your thoughts. Bipolar disorder also coincides with manic depression: a tendency to experience mood swings that take weeks, sometimes months, to go from one swing to the next. However, you can be happy one minute and down the next. But if not properly taking your meds every day, your manic episodes could last days... possibly weeks. When going through a manic episode, you have abnormal confidence in yourself. You never sleep, have racing thoughts, talk nonstop, and get very angry when people try to block your goals. You come up with unrealistic plans to become rich and famous and believe that your way is the only way, to the point you run up huge bills and live and act recklessly.

The first time I met Becky in person, she came to pick me up from my sober home. She was as tall as a model and as beautiful as one. We were driving to the beach, and she stopped at RJ's liquor store. I asked her why we were stopping there. She said, "To grab some Red Bulls." So, I waited for her in the car. She comes back out with a six-pack of Bud Lime-a-ritas and two nips of gin. I ask her, "Who are those for?" She says, "Us." I say,

"Becky, you know I'm in recovery, I can't drink." She says, "OMG, they're just wine coolers, a couple won't hurt." I say to her, "Becky, I live in a sober home." She says, "Don't worry, you're not going back home tonight." In Cape Cod, the white privileged act just as their label names them—privileged. We get to the beach, great weather, nice view. It looked like paradise. We lay on the beach towels and relax. She pulls out two wine coolers and goes to hand me one. I say, "Becky, I'm in recovery." She says, "Aren't you from Boston? I thought guys from the city know how to enjoy life?" I say, "What do you mean by that?" She says, "What's the problem? You're fresh out of prison after doing seven years. You're in Cape Cod, on the beach, the pandemic is over, and it's summertime. You're not going to enjoy it?" Damn, I'm sitting there… "stinking thinking" hitting me. I'm thinking, "Maybe she's right." Then she says, "This is what Cape Cod is all about, enjoying the beaches, the weather, the nightlife. You're going to miss the experience because you are in recovery?" I respond, "But I live in a sober home; if I catch a dirty, I can get kicked out." She says, "Don't worry, you can stay with me." Pause… self-reflection… damn, I threw six months of sobriety away for a rich piece of ass… SMFH.

Two nips and three wine coolers in, I'm feeling disgusted. I had let myself slip and fall to temptation. I feel defeated. We stop at Starbucks, and Becky speaks, "What's wrong?" I stay silent. She says, "Why are you so worried? It's okay." Then, "Do you want to see my house?" Unmindfully, I say, "Whatever you want to do." She starts laughing. Then she suddenly stops and says, "Oh shit!" I look at her and say, "What?" She says, "I think the cops are following us" (pause… first sign)… I look back to check, because being from the city, I know cops when I see them… none in sight. (Remember one of the key symptoms… seeing people that aren't really there.) I say, "Becky, you're bugging, there's no one behind us." She says, "I saw them, they are always behind me, following me." I say, "For what?" She responds, "Because my dad was a federal judge, and they're always keeping tabs on me." (Another symptom: believing that people are plotting against you.) I start thinking… WTF?

We're driving down Woods Hole Road, and a thought pops in my head: "Woods Hole?" If you know the Cape, Woods Hole is where you go to catch the ferry to Nantucket and Martha's Vineyard. To live in Woods Hole, you're either going to school for oceanography, or you're filthy rich. Becky lived in the smack center. We arrive at her home, and Becky basically has her own studio inside the family house. We go straight upstairs, and immediately she wants to have sex.

After sex, Becky's mom calls for her. This is when I started to wonder more; she's talking to Becky like a child. I'm thinking, "Wow, how nice it is to be rich, not having to worry about anything." From this moment to the next three weeks of my experience with Becky, I was taught a lot about the realities of "Rich White America."

This is what I also learned. When Becky was in PHP, she had recently been released from the psych ward for refusing to take her meds, which resulted in her going through a manic episode and her mother having to section her. I met her when she was stable. By the time I learned the truth about her, I really liked her. To this day, I haven't seen Becky in a couple of years. She blamed me for giving her too much confidence… which led to her next episode.

I was going through a downward spiral. I was drinking every day, going to the Raw Bar with Becky. I lost my job, ended up getting kicked out of the sober home, and was now living in hotels. However, Becky was spoiling me. I was living like I was rich. SHIT JUST GOT REAL. Becky was living a fantasy; she was in full-blown manic mode. My probation officer wanted me back in detox, but I was ducking her. Besides me losing my job and living in hotels trying to find another sober home, to be quite honest, I was enjoying this experience. Then it was brought to a halt.

Becky decided she wanted to spend the weekend in Boston, which was fine with me because I hadn't been there in a while. I got a chance to see my daughter, my nieces and nephews, and spend some time in the city. As soon as we hit the town, you should've seen Becky's face… priceless. First incident: Becky is running red lights and turning on no-turn-on-red signs, thinking she's still in Falmouth. I yell, "Becky!!!" She says, "What?" "I'm on federal probation, and I'm Black, and the cops know me here. You are not in Falmouth!! If they pull us over... you're going home, I'm going to jail!" She yells back, "Why are you so afraid of the cops?! The cops are your friends, they are on your side!" Oh... my... fucking... God! She then says, "Let's go downtown." I'm like, "Okay, sure." All I want is for her to park this car so we can get out and walk so I can feel safer. We're riding around looking for a parking spot. All of a sudden, she pulls to the side and tells me to wait in the car. First, she goes into Macy's. I'm sitting in the car for 45 minutes, thinking, "What is she doing?" She then pops up with a bag full of perfumes, clothes, and accessories. She is starting one of the other symptoms... running up bills. She then goes into a jewelry store. By this time, I've got my cigarettes, a half-pint of Hennessy, and a 40-bag of k-2, so I'm cool.

15 minutes later, she comes out and throws a bag on my lap and says, "Here, put those on." I go in the bag and pull out two gold chains. I say, "Becky, why did you buy these?" She says, "I want you to look like 50 Cent." I say, "What?" She starts yelling, "Why are you questioning me! I take care of you, just put the shit on!" I yell back, "Stop fucking talking to me like that!" All of a sudden, she pulls over and starts crying. I'm thinking, "WTF am I going through right now?" I say, "I'm sorry, Becky, please stop crying." She says, "I just wanted you to look like a rapper." Right then, I realized what's going on. Becky is living out her fantasy... dating a rapper! She stops crying, sits silent for five minutes, then says, "I'm sorry, I just went through a little breakdown, I'm fine now. We need to find a hotel." Then she starts smiling and pulls off. At this time, I know nothing about bipolar disorder, so I'm sitting, looking confused.

I tell her to find a hotel. Then I go into a trance. I'm thinking to myself, "Something is wrong, but I can't figure it out." Then I started thinking, "Maybe this is how all rich girls act," seeing that I've never had a rich girl before. As I snap out of it, Becky is getting out of the car, but I notice we are in front of the Ritz Carleton in Downtown Boston. I get out of the car and follow her in. She's booking a room for two days... TWO GRAND! I say, "Becky, are you nuts!?" Granted, I'm a Holiday Inn type of guy. The Ritz? This shit was fancy. We checked into the room, very nice. I can view the whole Boston Common through the window. We "break" the room in, then shower up to check out the nightlife.

Before we go out, I decided to roll up a jay of deuce. While I'm smoking, I notice that Becky had two packs of Pepto Bismol chews in her hand. I figured her stomach was bothering her, but what I saw next let me know... oh yeah, this girl is bugged the fuck out! Becky was eating the Pepto Bismol like they were Skittles! One by one. Then she opens the next pack. I ask her, "Becky... what the hell are you doing?! That's not candy!" She says, "They're good." I say, "Becky, you just ate a whole pack of laxatives." She yells back, "They are not laxatives!" I yell back, "They are!!" Then she says to me, "I'm the paramedic, you can't tell me anything about medicine!" (Symptom alert: when bipolar people go through a manic episode, they are always right.) So I say to her, "If you don't know that Pepto Bismol is a laxative, then you are the worst paramedic on the planet, and whoever hired you should be fired!" She just waves me off... and I don't waste any more breath.

The rest of the night was even more craziness. She was running more red lights, zooming through the town looking for a tattoo shop, and talking about getting a teardrop tattooed on her face. OMG... I had to really talk her out of it. She even tried to break into Fenway Park when it was closed! That night was a catastrophe. After almost three hours of begging her, I had finally convinced her to go back to the hotel.

I had to force her to eat, then monitor her because she was trying to throw it back up. Yeah, I forgot to tell you, she was also bulimic. She'll eat two French fries and swear to God she just gained ten pounds. Before we go to sleep, we have a nightcap, then I dozed off.

At about 4:00 a.m., I wake up. I roll over to get some vagina. Suddenly, Becky pops up out of the bed saying, "Holy shit!" I say, "What?" She yells, "There's shit everywhere!" I look around the room, thinking she's saying the room is messy… think again, lol. I say, "Becky, there's nothing on the floor." She says, "NO, I shit all over the place!" lol… I say, "What?!" She turns around, and what used to be two little pale butt cheeks were painted brown, lol. I lifted up the covers, and the side she was laying on had a big brown shit stain on the sheets. I started cracking up! I mimicked her, "I'm the paramedic, you can't tell me nothing about medicine"… dumbass! She is so embarrassed she tried to kick me out of the room naked. I joke, "I can't believe this… you shit yourself in the bed at the Ritz, lol." While she gets in the shower, I take the sheets off and redo the bed to make it look normal. She gets dressed. We leave, hit the highway, and headed straight back to Falmouth. Mind you, she was so embarrassed she didn't even care that we still had a whole day left in the room… $1,000 bucks down the drain.

On our way back to the Cape, Becky stopped at least four times to take a shit. The whole time I'm dragging her through the mud, she finally admits that she was wrong. Once we got back, she drops me off at the Admiralty Inn where I still had a day left on the room. She says, "I'm going home to take a nap." I say, "Cool, I'll call you in a few hours." Then she drives away.

Quick pause for a self-assessment. I've finally come to realize that denial has been a plague in my life, and it's time to step into reality. "IF IT LOOKS LIKE A DUCK, AND QUACKS LIKE A DUCK… IT'S A DUCK." At this point, I knew Becky was batshit crazy, but what I'm about to tell you next… put the icing on the cake.

I wake up from a nap two hours later and decide to call and check on Becky. I texted her first, "What's up"… no response. Then I video call her on Messenger. She answers. I notice immediately she's driving, and it looks like she's on the highway. I ask her, "Becky, where are you?" She says, "I'm on the highway." I say, "I see that, but where are you going?" She says, "I'm going to New York." I respond, "What? New York?… For what?" This cuckoo bird says, "I'm going to New York City to get signed."… Signed?… Quick pause… I also forgot to mention that Becky makes music. Rap music at that, and I take full responsibility for her thinking she's good enough to get signed, but when I tell you that this girl's music is horrible, I mean a five-year-old can put a better song together, but moving along… I say, "Becky, please turn around and come back. It doesn't work like that, you can't just bust into somebody's office talking about, 'sign me.'" She says, "Uhm, yes you can." I say, "Becky, no you can't, it doesn't work that way." She says, "I believe it does." Then I said to myself, "Oh my god, I'm really dealing with a fucking retard!" Now that I know all about bipolar disorder, I know she was going through a symptom—you come up with unrealistic plans to become rich and famous. But at that time, I didn't know any better. So I yell at her, "Becky! Turn the fucking car around and come back!!" She yells back, "No!! You need to learn how to live without me for a few days; I'm not your mother!!" I shoot back, "Becky, you don't even know where you're going. You're going to walk in the wrong place and get kidnapped." She says, "No, I'm not! Stop hating on me!" I say to myself, "WTF?" Now that I know, this was surety that she was going through a manic episode—the symptom of getting mad at me because I'm trying to block her goals. Now… I have no choice. I say to Becky, "If you don't turn around and come back, I'm calling your mother."… Fuck… I'm hoping I can figure out an alternative, because that bitch is the last one I'm trying to call. Becky's mom doesn't like me at all. I'm Black, I'm poor, and I'm an ex-con. As I told you before, Becky's late dad was a federal judge, so her mom is prejudiced towards convicted drug dealers and believes Becky deserves someone better than me. She doesn't even call me by my name; she calls me the "felon."

I get on Messenger and I find her sister, Daisy. I say to her, "Daisy, I don't know what's going on with Becky, but she is on her way to New York talking about she is going there to get signed." She replies, "Hey, James, thanks for informing us." I ask her, "Can you please tell me what's wrong with her?" First she asks me, "Did she say anything about hurting herself?" I say no. Then she hits me with the meat and potatoes… "James, Becky has bipolar disorder. She's had it since she was a kid, and she stopped taking her meds." I immediately googled bipolar disorder… oh shit! That explains it! She then says, "Becky was stable when she was taking her meds, but when she started dealing with you, she felt as though she didn't need them anymore, so she hasn't took them for four days, and now she is going through an episode, and it is important that we get her help." Thankfully, Becky's family has a brownstone in Manhattan, and they have someone renting it. So they coerced Becky to go to the brownstone, and her mom gets her sectioned into a psych hospital.

To sum it all up, when I lost Becky, I hit rock bottom. My PO violated me, and I ended up back in jail. Becky is straight; she is now stable and resides in Florida. Now that I'm aware of her illness, I look at Becky as a learning experience.

I learned a lot from Becky: money doesn't solve all problems. There are so many adults like Becky who have co-dependents because they are not mentally stable enough to take care of themselves. They have no control over their lives. Becky's mother controls every aspect of Becky's life: where she lives, her finances, her relationships—everything… and Becky is 33 years old. I hope that one day Becky and people like her will be able to shake this disorder so they know how it feels to have the freedom to make their own choices, to take full control of their own lives.

As for me, do I blame Becky for my relapse? At first, yes. Now that I have more wisdom and I've learned how to accept reality, no. It was ultimately my choice to drink those wine coolers and those nips. And furthermore, it was my decision to keep on indulging to the point I eventually ended up biting the dust… pure reality.

Chapter 5

Okay, now I'm going to take a break from my step work and break down the business side of recovery. In doing so, it's possible that some may get offended by what I'm about to teach the people who are unaware of the vicious reality of how recovery plays a significant role in fueling the economy.

I'm going to break this chapter into categories for the purpose of individualizing each step in the cycle of recovery, explaining in detail how different industries such as medical, real estate, pharmaceuticals, and even churches benefit from it.

Figure 5.1 is basically an outline of the continuous recycle of recovery. In "Rational Steps To Recovery: When A.A. Doesn't Work," a book by Ellis and Velten, it explains how 20 percent of the people in recovery fail. Do you think this is a coincidence, or do you think it was planned to be that way?

The spin cycle of recovery viewed in Figure 5.1 is broken down into four phases: detox, treatment, recovery maintenance, and lastly, relapse.

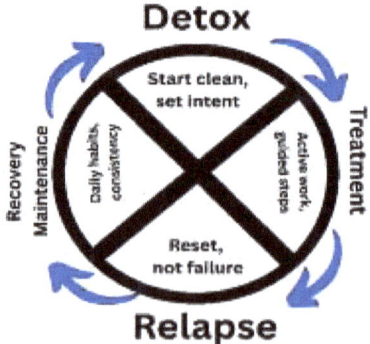

DETOX

This is the first phase: detoxing, or cleansing your body of a substance. A detox is where you go to safely recover from the withdrawal of alcohol or opioids. They usually consist of a medical staff that monitors your symptoms with a medicated process called a "protocol." Depending on what you're detoxing from determines which protocol you are on. For example, I was withdrawing from alcohol, so I was placed on an alcoholic protocol. Alcohol protocols last up to seven days. The medication provided is usually Librium, Viseril, and Phenobarbital. Opioid protocols are longer, usually taking up to 10 to 12 days. You can pick from two types of opioid protocols: either a methadone type or a suboxone type.

Business Side of It

Depending on what type of insurance you have, that determines how fast you get a bed. Private insurance holders get beds faster than state-funded insurance holders. Detoxes make their money based on keeping their beds full. Most types of insurance plans cover detox, but not all plans cover further treatment. You have some addicts or alcoholics who constantly go through a detox because a detox will admit you 100 times if need be. Why? Because your insurance will cover it. The fucked-up part about it is this: The drugs they use to help you through withdrawal are called Benzodiazepines, or by the street name, Benzos. Benzos are addictive. Maintenance drugs, or MATs such as suboxones or methadone, are also addictive. So, quite frankly, detoxes help you kick a substance with a substance. You go into detox with a habit and leave with a habit.

TREATMENT

The next phase (if your insurance covers it) is further treatment. You have short-term treatment and long-term treatment. For example, Emerson, which runs through Gosnold Health, is a 28-day program, which is short-term. Foundations, however, is a 90-day program, which is long-term. Inpatient days usually start with the thought for the day. You read the thought of the day from a book, then you share what the reading meant to you. After that, throughout the day, you have different groups, such as relapse prevention, cognitive behavioral skills, and health awareness. The day then ends with final thoughts where you go around the group and everyone shares how their day went. At the end, everyone circles around and recites the serenity prayer. Outpatient is basically PHP (Partial Hospitalization Program) through Zoom, meeting with a treatment specialist once a week, and a mental health counselor once a month.

Business Side of It

Depending on what your insurance covers determines what kind of treatment you are eligible for, and how prestigious the treatment center is determines the cost. For example, Gosnold On The Cape is probably the most prestigious treatment company in Massachusetts. When I first entered treatment, Cataumet, Emerson, and the Miller House were owned by them. Now it's just Emerson. But Miller House only took private insurance; it was a 90-day treatment program. So, basically, they only took people with money. The only reason I was lucky to go to the Miller House is because the feds paid for me to be there, and when the feds pay for you, you're worth three times more than a person with private insurance. Other facilities like SSTAR in Fall River, High Point in New Bedford, and Dimock St in Boston are state-owned, which means less expensive. Also, when you go to an inpatient program, you automatically get a psych evaluation. They diagnose you with mental health disorders, then prescribe you mental health medications. Who cashes in? Pharmaceutical companies, because your insurance pays for the prescription.

Outpatient is more affordable. Most insurance plans, such as MassHealth, don't have a problem paying for IOP (Intensive Outpatient Program). It's a 3-hour program for two days a week, with co-payments on psych meds and talking to a therapist once a month. The sad part of it all... out of 100 people, 50 are going to drop out before they even complete inpatient. Out of the 50 that do complete it, 20 of them will relapse almost immediately after, leaving 30 that will continue with their recovery. The other 30 percent will fall right back into the spin cycle.

RECOVERY MAINTENANCE

After you've finished treatment, meaning you are one of the 50, you're now in the process of maintaining your recovery. This usually consists of living in a sober living, a structured living environment where everyone who lives there is focusing on recovery and working on being productive members of society. You faithfully attend N.A/A.A meetings and become a part of the recovery community, joining committees and doing commitments, which is basically going to different facilities and sharing your story on what made you choose sobriety over substance abuse.

Business Side of It

This is where ordinary people like you and me can make a pretty penny off the name of recovery! As I said, sober homes are structured living environments where everyone who lives there is focused on recovery and becoming productive members of society. Who are the owners of these structured living environments? Homeowners! Normal people like you and me. In Falmouth alone, there are about 20 or more different sober homes. Yet still, the demand for beds outweighs the supply substantially. Most people leaving treatment plan on going to sober homes out of fear that if they go home, the possibility of them relapsing is greater. To give you an example of how lucrative owning a sober home is: I know this old man named T. He actually owned the first sober home I lived in when I left treatment, and he's in recovery. Anyhow, he owns two sober homes on the same street, a male one and a female one. There are 11 guys living in the male house and 11 women living in the female house—a total of 22 beds. He gets 200 bucks a week for each bed. That's 2,200 bucks a week per house, a total of 4,400 bucks a week. Now, times that by four, that's 17,600 dollars a month. Now, expenses. Let's say he's paying two grand apiece per month for mortgage, a grand a month for utilities, 500 bucks a month for supplies, and we're going to say… two grand a month for house managers, a total of four grand. It sums up to a total of 9,500 bucks a month, leaving you with 8 grand a month… all profit. Both homes pay for themselves. The beauty of it? The demand for beds is so high, your homes will always be filled.

This is where I might catch some backlash, lol. Fuck it, though. The truth isn't always peaches and cream. Almost all the A.A. meetings I've attended were conducted in a church. Every meeting I've ever been to passes a collection plate around. This money is supposedly used to pay for big books and also to pay for renting out the space for meetings. Who are you paying the rent to? The Church. So even the pastor makes a dollar in the name of recovery!

RELAPSE

Relapse is the graveyard phase of recovery, where 70 percent of us end up. Notice I said "us." We lost the battle, whether it was from temptations or triggers. Rational Steps to Quitting Alcohol calls it Rational Emotive Therapy… or R.E.T., which follows the ABCs. Activating events are normally a place, a person, or a mental state that gives you the idea to drink. Beliefs are what you tell yourself to persuade yourself to drink. Then the consequences… Relapse.

The Business Side of it

The business of recovery depends on that 70 percent. Why? Because without relapse, there's no need for a detox or further treatment. Imagine if everyone who decided to recover from substance abuse actually remained sober and never relapsed. Recovery centers would go out of business, and hundreds of jobs and billions of dollars would be lost. So do you honestly think recovery centers sincerely care about your recovery? As long as relapse exists, the spin cycle will live forever.

Chapter 6

Step 6: We're entirely ready to have God remove all these defects of character.

My character defects usually end up with me hurting myself and not realizing the pain I'm causing to the people in my life. Every failure, every downfall, every jail sentence, and every breakup were all brought upon me from the negative and irrational choices I've made in life, deriving from alcohol abuse.

Now that I'm working on my belief system and my relationship with my creator, I've been utilizing my subconscious thoughts and honestly admitting to myself that my pattern of wrong choices in life was caused by me being ignorant of what's right and what's wrong. Before I was enlightened, drinking every day was considered normal. Selling drugs was normal. Hearing gunshots and witnessing overdoses on the streets? Normal. These are so-called "normal" things that happen in the environment that I come from. Now that my eyes are open and my mind is clear of a substance, I realize that the way I was living, and what I thought was normal, was actually fucked up.

I love and respect my father. He took care of me regardless of whether people think it was the morally correct way or not. However, the way he raised and nurtured me wasn't normal. My dad hustled to be what and where he wanted to be. He instilled this hustler mentality into me. He took care of me the way he saw fit. There were times when I didn't see my dad for weeks. There were times my dad would be around other women. When I got older, I realized that my dad was a player. He had other women, but my mom was the queen. My mom was the complete opposite of my dad's "other" women. Now, before I continue, I ask you, please don't judge my pops. My dad was taught by my grandpa to be this way. He was raised to think that this way of life was "normal." So, when he had a son, he truly believed that this was the way you were supposed to raise him.

My pop's philosophy was, as long as you take care of home, however you choose to live your life is how you see fit. My dad had two lives. My family was his backbone. My mom was the purity in his life. She taught him about credit, going on vacations, and doing normal people shit. My mom had street in her as well, but her love for God and the positive nurturing she'd given to us was more important to her than my dad's street activities. Plus, my mom was a college grad. However, dad also had a street family. He had a "street" woman who participated in his drug dealing enterprise. She was his "Bonnie," his main "runner." She was the one who did the running around to get the money that my dad used… to take care of me and my family.

I gave you this brief description of my dad's lifestyle to further justify why I thought and lived the way I did before I stepped to reality. My dad was my role model. The way he had raised me was the way I had thought you were supposed to live. When I normally have relationships with women, depending on my motive, they are either the opposite of me or they're my sidekick. I would have a "square" woman and a "street" woman.

My dad also spoiled me rottenly. Like me in the present, then, my dad used to take frequent trips to "heartbreak hotel"… jail. However, he used to always show me the difference between him being here and not. For example, dad would disappear for two weeks; my mom and I would look for him, but couldn't find him. Suddenly, he would pop up. Him and my mom would argue for the whole day, but by the next day he would be out of the doghouse (lol). Me, on the other hand, he would take me everywhere and buy me so much shit that I would totally forget he was gone for the last two weeks.

This same method of parenting I would later use with my daughter. When I'm not in jail, I spoil my daughter rottenly. She never hears the word "no" because I feel as though I owe her for the time that I wasn't there. So, I will try to make up for it. I only wish I had thought then that my daughter would've rather had me in her life completely, than thinking money and material things solve everything. I would've focused on being a full-time dad instead of thinking I can just buy her love. This way of thinking is a defect that I greatly want to remove because I want my daughter to love me, for me, and not for what I can do for her.

My dad taught me how to be a man in a dysfunctional way. In my environment, dysfunctional is normal… I had inherited this "normal."

When you enjoy pain, you are considered a "masochist." For the last ten years I feel as though I deserve that title because no matter how aware I am of the consequences I face from me drinking and being careless, I drink, get caught up, then kick myself in the ass the next day when I'm sober and realize I did some dumb shit. Prime example…

Most… no… ALL my drug cases that I've ever caught, I was intoxicated and practically gave myself to the police. Being careless, doing dirt while not being in the right state of mind. Walking around the streets, drunk with crack in my pocket. Or even worse, what I served 90 months in the feds for. Selling drugs to strangers who turn out to be federal informants. Or how about this boneheaded mistake… I did a year for violating probation because I had decided to argue with the police in Falmouth hospital forgetting, due to being intoxicated, that I had 11 bags of crack in my pocket. I had a dumb habit: every time I got drunk, I would put my crack in my lighter pocket, and every time I got arrested for possession of crack, that's exactly where they would find it… every time.

The defect of me drinking and doing dirt at the same time has been so detrimental to my life it's been destroying me and taking everything and everyone I held dear to my life. By me facing this reality, I also accept the fact that I gave myself to the feds. Even though the sentence I was given for one sale of crack was inhumane and filled with disparity, I gave them the opportunity to violate me the way they did. If I was thinking rationally and logically without the influence of the bottle, I wouldn't have done business with a stranger. That one fuck-up caused me to be federal property for the following ten years of my life. A piece of crack… not even a gram, I suffered for almost a whole decade for.

Me asking my creator to remove my defects is one thing. I know I must do my part as well. I know if he sees my desire to change, my persistence at living the steps, whether I slip and get back up, I'm going to try again until I get it right. I will receive my blessings through giving back what I get from living as righteous as I possibly can. I know that everything begins with a thought, and that thought turns into action. However, the way you choose to think will determine the way you act. Power granted by your creator.

Now, back to the situation at hand… step work. Another resource which proved to be very insightful to me is a book by Allen Berger PhD called "12 Stupid Things That Mess Up Recovery." The main stupid thing that hits me in that book is number six: Not making amends. It states, "To develop a strong foundation for recovery, it is essential that we accept full responsibility for our harmful behavior and that we attempt to repair the damage that we have caused in our relationships with family, friends, and loved ones." It also states that "It's one of the greatest challenges in recovery but yet essential if you are going to enjoy all the benefits and promises of recovery and wish to re-establish trust."

To be honest, I've never read the Big Book from cover to cover. A lot of the knowledge and techniques I've obtained on recovery come from multiple sources, such as the latter. I've been running from step work due to the fact that a lot of it is faith-based, and furthermore, I didn't feel comfortable sharing my life in-depth with a sponsor. Now that I have the wisdom and courage to accept my mistakes and to focus on changing what I can, I decided to share my life with the world. So, if you are reading this book… you are now my sponsor, lol.

In making amends, be aware that in the realities of accepting your wrongdoing, some people will forgive you, and some won't. Just know that the sole purpose of apologizing is not forgiveness, but for clearing your conscience. Some amendments you might make reluctantly, feeling like that person doesn't deserve an apology. In that case, you take an honest, moral inventory of yourself. In doing so, you usually realize the things that you might've said or done to contribute to the fallout, and you apologize for the role you played in it.

So this is the chapter that I make amends to those whom I've done harm to in my lifetime, whether it was with words or bad deeds. This is the part of recovery that I feared the most. Now it's time to face the beast.

The first amend I would like to make is to my creator. For not giving him my utmost loyalty and embracing the reason he put me on this earth. For denying my calling to be a leader of good, and instead using my gift to promote negative influence, and not choosing the right side of the war between good and evil. I've come to learn and fully understand why every bad deed I've tried to carry out throughout my life crumbled. You show me tremendously the possibilities I have when I choose to do what I know is right. You also have put me through a lot of pain by severely punishing me for making bad decisions, as a way of deterring me from making further ones.

As I ask for your forgiveness, I would also like to thank you for the many blessings you have bestowed upon me: my beautiful daughter, my grandson, my nieces and nephews, and the privilege to wake up and live another day. Giving me the power to understand and identify the people whom you have put in my life for a reason versus the ones you test me with. And furthermore, having the wisdom to know the difference.

Creator, I'm not perfect and still have ways to go to fully embrace my true calling. I just humbly ask that you please continue to protect me and my loved ones and continue to show me the ways to happiness. AMEN.

The next person I would like to make amends to is me. Yep, I'm apologizing to myself for living a lie. I'm what you call a pseudo-hoodlum, meaning I made myself into a street cat. I never knew how it felt to struggle. Besides growing up in the projects, I had a pretty good childhood. As I told you, my mother was a medical assistant at an AIDS hospice, and my pops had a master's in drugonomics. The landlord never evicted us, I never went without heat, and Christmas never missed my house. I was fortunate to have both parents in my life. In fact, my home was a hangout spot on holidays. All my friends would come to my house because whatever new video game or system came out, they knew I had it.

As for education, I'm a pretty smart dude. It's not a coincidence that I'm good at writing literature. As a matter of fact, I believe I could've excelled in journalism. When I was in middle school, I attended James P. Timilty Middle School in Boston. I wrote a piece on my best friend, Terrance Milton, who, to this day, helped me get through the time my mom got her leg amputated due to diabetes. I was presented with an award for writing that essay from the President of the United States at that time, Bill Clinton… big facts.

I say all of that to say this: I lived the street life by choice, not by force. I had enough influence in my teenage years to have become someone way more productive in society than I am today. But due to brief moments where my inability to not care about what or how my neighborhood peers thought of me, and pride, I chose instead to prove to them (my homies) that I was just like them. This led to me living a life of crime and spending the majority of my young adulthood in prison.

The humility and shame are so unbearable at times, I'm too embarrassed to even speak to certain people in my life who had high expectations of me. I have positive friends who chose the right path and grew up in the same conditions as I did. Where you live or where you were raised doesn't ultimately define who you are. One of my friends I grew up with came from a rough background. People had him doomed from the start. We came from the same neighborhood. With dedication and determination not to become another statistic, he defeated the odds, ended up going to college, playing professional basketball in Europe, and is now working as a correctional officer, making an honest living, collecting a pension, and enjoying life.

Fortunately, I've now accepted the fact that all of my downfalls were self-inflicted and aided by my choice to abuse alcohol. I'm now 40 years old and old enough to know better but still young enough to change and make a difference. The great thing about learning how to become unconditionally honest with yourself and gaining acceptance is that your choice to change is internal. Meaning, if you really want to turn your life around, you will do it, and no outside forces would be able to stop you.

The most hurtful part of making amends, at least to me, is apologizing to the ones that are no longer here on this earth. Both of my parents, along with my brother, died while I was incarcerated. My mom died in 2014. She was the matriarch of my family. I was her baby boy. I was the one that was supposed to make the family proud, but I failed her. Instead, I broke my mother's heart by choosing the street life. She didn't raise me to be that way. I didn't get a chance to talk to my mom, nor was I able to bury her when she passed due to the feds' inhumane decision to not let prisoners attend their immediate families' funerals. In fact, the last time I laid eyes on my mother was in a federal courtroom where she had to listen to your honorable Judge Dennis Saylor sentence me to 90 months in prison for a $40 piece of crack.

I'm sorry, Mommy… for not being there when you needed me the most and for not living up to the expectations you had for me. The creator said, "Honor your mother and your father so that your days are longer upon this earth." If that's the case, I know my days are numbered. I blame myself for your death. I was supposed to give you my kidney. You could've probably lived long enough for me to see you, hug you, and tell you I love you at least one last time. If I could turn my life in, in exchange to hear your voice again, I would. Just know that you left a God on this earth. Not a perfect one, but one you taught well enough to use his gift of being a natural leader for good. Thank you, Mom, for giving me the heart and the ability to care for others, to not judge people by their vices, but instead by the content of their character. I must admit that sometimes it frustrates me that I care for others so much that I'm vulnerable to being taken advantage of—a character trait I inherited from you. It's a gift and a curse. But you also instilled in me to fight for what's right and never back down from adversity. Thanks, Mom, for the unconditional love you had for me whether I was right, wrong, or indifferent. I love you, and I hope you accept my apology and enjoy everlasting peace in paradise.

My pops were the example of how you take care of your family, as far as I'm concerned. He had a "by any means necessary" type of attitude when it came to putting food on the table. My dad was everything to me growing up. Most of my friends didn't have dads in their lives. I was fortunate. Although my dad taught me a lot about being a man, he did it in a dysfunctional kind of way. All my dad knew was the hustle and bustle of the streets. He dropped out in the 4th grade. Before he came to Boston with my grandmother, Mary Dockery, he was born in South Carolina. He practically raised himself, but he had a gift. Accumulating money became so natural to him that it was like drinking water out of a faucet. My mom taught me how to work hard and get an education; on the other hand, my pops taught me the ins and outs of hustling. Unfortunately, but at the same time fortunately... pops won. It was unfortunate because it added to my resume of a life of crime. But it was fortunate because he taught me how to survive in any element. In my early adulthood, there were times when pops got locked up and I had to step up to the plate. At 18, I had to man up and be there for my mom to help maintain the family.

I was blessed to see my father before he died. I knew my dad was sick and on his way out. When my mom died, it took a toll on my pops, shit... and everyone else in the family. But for him, he had lost his rock, his best friend, the one who kept him strong. He was fighting heart problems and, worst of all, prostate cancer. When I was sent to the prerelease, I was able to go see my father and spend some time, then my dumbass got sent back to prison because I blew positive in the breathalyzer for alcohol. So once again, I couldn't bury my parent, unhonorable... days cut even shorter.

Dad, I want to say I'm sorry for not sending you to mommy the proper way. I know both of you are staring down at me right now, cussing me out for being a fuck-up again, but I just want you to know that I'm working on self… one day at a time. Thank you for teaching me the art of survival. Thank you for showing me that regardless of how you live your life, family is everything, and by any means necessary, you do what you have got to do to maintain it, even if that means taking risks. When mommy died, I asked you to please fight and do not die on me while I'm in the joint. You fought and stayed alive long enough to lay eyes on your baby boy a few more times before going to mommy. I love you, and I hope you also accept my apology and enjoy an everlasting life.

Chapter 7

The creator really works in mysterious ways. The year 2021 ended for me in the worst way. My brother died in prison from a fentanyl overdose. To make matters worse, I was two units away from him, in the same jail when it happened.

I say he works in mysterious ways because if the events that led to me ultimately ending up in the same jail as him wouldn't have ever happened, I would've never seen my brother one last time before he passed. Everything happens for a reason. I was supposed to go to jail. I truly believe that. For three reasons. One, to see my brother, hug him, and drink two cups of coffee with him for one last time. Furthermore, for him to have the opportunity to apologize to me for the way he treated me in the world due to his horrendous opioid addiction. My brother taught me tough love. He used to tell me I was too nice, that "being nice is gonna get you killed." The streets are mean. My brother was a great protector; I ran around the streets with immunity because of him. But when he was in full-blown addict mode, my brother was a vicious, scary, murderous motherfucker who would do anything to feed his addiction. Did I fear him? Absolutely. Did I have unconditional love for him… even more than myself at times.

Bro, I just want you to know I understood everything you were going through. We both lost mommy and didn't get to say goodbye. We both failed mommy and grieved by trying to drown the pain with a substance. You were a superhero to me, and I am proud to have you as a brother, whether right, wrong, or indifferent. I just want you to know that I apologize for not being the opposite of you, because if I was a better little brother, I would've done my best to help you instead of enabling you. I will continue to be an uncle to your children and grandchildren you left behind. Although Noonies is grown with children, he will always be little Noonies to me. You also created an intelligent, strong daughter who's determined to be successful, and the next generation: Big Boy, Gizmo, Nyla, and Kenjoy. I embrace the duty of being the elder of our family. I love you, my brother's keeper.

Now for the other two reasons. To get these people out of my life and come home a free man, mentally prepared to make progress in the right direction. And lastly, to sit my ass down and write this book.

On March 19th, 2005, the most precious person I ever created came into my life: my lil' mommas, Shaniya Dockery. Point blank, I have to make amends to her for not being the greatest dad I could've possibly been. I owe her the world and intend to give it to her. The consequences of me going to prison did a great number on our relationship. I missed her first steps, her first day of school, her elementary and middle school graduation, and a few other milestones in her life that a father should've been there for. I know my daughter loves me unconditionally. I know she has a perception of me that I vow to change. I just know that in order for me to fully recover and enjoy life, I have to involve myself with my daughter. I want you to know, mommas, that I love you more than life itself. I owe you everything, and I vow to do my best to make you prouder of being a Dockery. I'm grateful and blessed to make it to your high school graduation and witness you go off to experience young adulthood. And know that as long as I'm breathing, your dad will always be here for you.

As for your mother, I apologize to her for leaving her out there to raise you alone. I was young and dumb when I had you and thought running the streets was cool as long as I provided for you. In and out of prison, leaving your mom out there to take care of you and getting mad because she had to do and be with who she had to in order to fill my shoes. I thank her for taking care of you to the best of her abilities, and applaud her for overcoming the obstacles she was faced with. Just know that regardless of me and your mother's differences, I wish her nothing but good blessings.

Friends, how many of us have them... Friends... ones you can depend on? Whodini... a classic. He was on to something, though. How many of your friends are actually your friends? Ones you know that will never switch up and be there for the bad times just as much as the good ones. I am fortunate enough to have some pretty good friends in my life. Ones who supported me through the seven and a half years. Actually, I was so embarrassed of going back to prison, even though it was a short stint, that I haven't even called nor communicated with any of them out of humility. One of my childhood friends, however, with words, I fucked up our relationship. This amend will be short and straight to the point. Because before I decided to write this book, when I was free, I tried to apologize to this man twice and he refused it. This will be the third and last time. He accepts it, God bless. He doesn't, still love him, but as long as I'm right with my creator, I'm comfy in my skin.

Listen, Knucks, when I came home, I was going through some real shit. My mental health was not there. I said things to you that were pretty hurtful and called you out your name. I didn't mean that shit. But at the end of the day, my loyalty is and always will be the same. You held me down when I was at the bottom. When I called you, you came through. I'm grateful to have you as a friend. On some real shit, my nigga… I'm just upset because you know me well enough to understand that when I was going through that fucked up situation. But for the record… I'm standing on this… I tell you a nigga running around slandering your name, you make it out to me slandering you? Naw, bro, that label is worse than any label you can possibly be given. I wouldn't ever give you that label unless I truly knew you were. I love you, my nigga, and always will. I never got a chance to congratulate you and Rita for the lil one. So congrats, bro. I hope you accept this last time apology so we can put the band back together. If not, I wish you and the family nothing but happiness, my nigga. And that's from the heart.

I end this chapter humbly asking my creator to guide me in the right direction of removing my shortcomings. I understand and accept the fact that change doesn't come from just bowing my head and asking for it. I have to play my part and dedicate myself to fixing my flaws in order to grow in my recovery. Acceptance is a major ally to the word humility.

Even though I'm humiliated by it, I accept the fact that it is my fault I ended back up in jail. My irrational thoughts led me to making stupid choices. Choices and mistakes are different. Mistakes are things said or done by accident. Choices are ultimately made before that action takes place. So due to my irrational thoughts and belief that when I think I have control over my life, I can drink alcohol, I make bad choices over and over again, which ends in bad results. My first acceptance of humility is when I decided to embrace the first step: I am powerless over alcohol, and my life has become unmanageable.

Chapter 8

Before I go forward with my step work, I would like to take a moment to give a motivational speech to the young boys running around in the streets just like I chose to do when I was a lad. Be advised that some of the content I use in this chapter may be considered explicit to some. If you weren't born and raised in the ghetto, never been locked up, or ever had to deal with the harsh realities of being a Black man born into a situation that was destined for you to fail, then this isn't for you. If you can think outside of the box, then proceed to read. But if you are ignorant to the matter, feel free to skip this chapter.

Young boy, I'm not your father, I'm not a role model, and although I'm working on being a positive figure, I'm not fully there yet. Take this time for what it's worth, to let this shit manifest in your head, or you can let it go in one ear and out the other. THE ODDS ARE AGAINST YOU. This society was designed to destroy us since the beginning of American history. These motherfuckers do not care about you. Every chance they get they show you that your life does not matter to them. A month ago, I witnessed a young white man get a not guilty verdict on all charges after he shot three people in the middle of the street with an AK-47 during a Black Lives Matter rally. But yet you can get 10-plus years? The oppressor will take your life away in a courtroom with the quickness and lose no sleep over it. And don't get it twisted, the oppressor comes in all shapes, sizes, and colors. As a matter of fact, a lot of times it'll be the ones that look like you to treat you worse than the ones that don't. You have to learn the identity of your enemy. They are not from the street next to you, or the nearest housing development… they are the ones in suits and ties that control the checks and balances of the economy. They control the cops, the prosecutors, and the judges.

The game is officially over. The rules are no longer honored. The risk outweighs the reward by a landslide. The same dudes you grew up playing in the sandbox with could be the one to give your life away. Connects are now giving up workers. Gangsters are now telling on connects and still roaming the streets with no worries because, yeah, they snitched, but they will also kill you.

I'm not judging you, nor am I trying to tell you what to do, lil homies. I'm just trying to teach you how to execute risk assessment in your everyday life. Meaning, before you take action in any decision you make, first analyze the scenario. For instance, if you choose to go along with whatever risk you're deciding to take... what is the rate of success? Is it a greater chance you succeed? Or fail? Next, how many times have you taken this risk? And if multiple times, did you ever succeed?

If you're a drug dealer, and you really be in the trenches, the odds are against you substantially to the point it's not IF you get caught, but more so WHEN. My mother used to tell me the cops aren't worried about catching you because one day you will slip up. You can get away 100 times, they only need to catch you once. At first, I used to think that's 100 to 1 odds in my favor, shit... not realizing that WHEN they do catch you, they're going to give you enough time to make up for the 99 times you got away with it.

That's fucked up, but it's reality. When you catch the first felony, you knock yourself out of the race of life. You can never own a firearm or work a government or state job unless it's the labor force. You will never work for a Fortune 500 company, unless you create one. Once you enter the matrix your chances of recidivating (going back and forth to prison) are high.

If I had the wisdom to know what I know now, I would've made a lot of different choices, but wouldn't we all have? I'm trying to prevent you from having to say "IF" and instead make the right choices now. We are willing to kill each other over street signs and housing developments we can't even hang out in anymore. Most beefs either started over some stupid shit or have been going on for so long your generation doesn't even know what it started over. The oppressor loves it, though. They love to sit back and watch us exterminate each other. Whether it's us killing each other, them killing us in the middle of the streets, or murdering us in the courtrooms, we get rid of ourselves for them. To leave you with something to think about: Do you think it's a coincidence that all the majorly predominant Black cities in America—Chicago, Baltimore, D.C., Philly—are always the top murder capitals every year? Do you honestly believe if the oppressor wanted to decrease the number of homicides in these cities, they wouldn't have been declared a state of emergency and had the military patrolling until they detained almost everyone suspected of contributing to the 500-plus murders per year these cities accumulate? Absolutely not… it's in the plans. Sit back and let them kill each other.

In a nutshell, we must know our value, our true worth to our people. My favorite movie of all time is Planet of the Apes. Not because of the action, but because of the message behind it. If you consider yourself a great mind, with your eyes open, and no longer a part of the deaf, dumb, and blind, I advise you to watch all four of the Planet of the Apes movies and get the message. However, I'm going to give it to you briefly.

Apes, just like humans, come in all shapes, sizes, and colors. You have chimps, silverbacks, and orangutans. You have aggressive ones, and some that are passive but mean if you push them. When it's all said and done, however, they are all apes. It took the leader, Caesar, to come to the pen, realize he was a part of an oppressed species, get all of the apes to band together, and teach them—from the toughest silverback to the smartest orangutan—that if we all come together as one, we cannot be broken and can rise from oppression.

That was the message to us as a people. The oppressor works adamantly every day, since the beginning of civilization, to keep us separated systemically. They know how powerful we would become if we smartened up and realized how powerful we are as one. The oppressor wouldn't be able to control it. They fear that day ever comes, to the point they came up with a plan 300 years ago to prevent that from happening. And when a "Caesar" pops up… they get rid of him.

The movie reminds the oppressor and the one percent of the world that if they allow us to learn our identity and unite to become one, this is what will happen. There's an old saying, "If you want to hide something from a Black person, put it in a book." These motherfuckers are so cocky they put it right in front of your face now; we are just too fucking dumb to notice it.

And don't get it fucked up... just as much as we need our "Caesars," we also need our "Kobas," for the times when violence is the only option respected.

Chapter 9

Step 10: Continued to take personal inventory, and when we were wrong, promptly admitted it.

When I further take moral inventory of myself, and become more comfortable with who I am, another characteristic I embrace with acceptance is my fascination with women. I have so many Becky-type stories stacked up from my time in Falmouth, I can literally write a whole book about it, Becky was just the most significant.

I'm addicted to vagina. White, black, Hispanic, Asian, all shapes and sizes. All my life, since the age of nine, I've been a freak, more so a ladies' man. I've always put more "concern" with the "satisfaction" or approval of women more than my own. The first time I "concerned" myself with a women's "satisfaction," I was nine years old in a closet with my boys' older sister. She told me to stick my tongue in it and just lick… since that day, I've mastered the craft of "concerning" myself with the "satisfaction" of all women.

The negative side to that is I had a tough time choosing the right one to fall in love with verses the ones to just take for what it's worth. I will never forget the first time the love bug hit me… Sonjia W… middle school. She is now a fashion designer doing great for herself.

To be real, though, the next time I fell in love was with my daughter's mother. However, we went through some crazy shit at the end of it. We had a decent relationship. We were just young, I went to jail, and while I was there, she did some fucked up shit. I used to think that one day we would be a family again, but some shit just isn't meant to happen.

Which brings me to now. I've been a man whore ever since. And my pick with women as far as the ones to keep, and then ones to run away from has been so fucked up, I could no longer tell the difference. I've had some great women since then, but I always seem to fuck it up by not being able to keep my penis in my pants. It's like I'm attracted to train wrecks... worst of all... train wrecks in recovery.

Momma Martha had a phrase she used to call them... dented cans. From the first day she met me, she knew I was a ladies' man. I have a habit that I'm known for in Gosnold detox: every time I check into detox, I leave with a female... every single time. To the point the recovery assistants used to ask me, "Which one are you leaving with this time?"

Martha used to say to me, "James, you must stop dealing with all the dented cans. They are in recovery, super sensitive, and vulnerable right now, so if you're not truly into them and just want a piece of ass, trust me, it's not worth the headaches." Martha is what you call an old-school dented can. She used to be a wild one in her day. She's 30-plus years clean now, and so comfortable with life she has no problem letting it be known. In fact, she'll tell you, "If I had as many pricks coming out of me as I had going inside of me in my younger days, I would've been a porcupine," lol. At 60-plus years old, she still looked good. And if she wasn't married, I'd probably would've been the next needle, lol.

She also taught me the difference between A.A. and N.A. A.A. is more of an older folk, laid-back setting. N.A., however, is the young crowd. That's where all the girls are. Going through recovery, getting healthy, dressing to impress, and super horny. They say when a female is recovering from opioid abuse, three things happen: they get thick, they eat a lot, and their hormones reach a thousand.

Momma Martha told me to stay away from N.A. meetings. She said, "For one, you're Black and handsome, so you're like an exotic piece of meat out here." She then says, "Two, most girls in N.A. are young. They go there with the tightest leggings on to show off their camel toe to guys like you. They are trying to be the first one to screw the new kid." It's like high school all over again. Finally, she tells me, "James, you don't want to try all the shirts. You want to find the right one. In due time when it's supposed to happen, you will find that person that has dignity and self-respect. Then you'll be able to appreciate them more, instead of them just being a piece of ass in the long run."

In recovery, they say that you're not supposed to be in a relationship for the first year of sobriety. You're supposed to be working on self, and relationships get in the way of your recovery. At first, I used to think that it was ridiculous. Me? No women for a whole year? No way! Now that I'm a little more aware, the key word is "relationship." It never says anything about "friendships." I know you're probably thinking, "that's a loophole!" No, that's you being perfectly honest with yourself and that significant other.

Let's say you meet someone and the two of you hit it off right away. She's sober, has her priorities in order, and has never been in recovery. She shows you that she genuinely cares for your best interests. However, you are in recovery and have been clean for six months, but you feel you can't move forward for another six months because of the "one year rule." She knows what she wants and is ready to settle with you, so you must explain your situation, right? Honestly, I think a year is too long; six months is more reasonable. I'm not saying to rush into anything you're not ready for, but sometimes we let good things and opportunities pass us by while trying to be too perfect. Then we waste time on someone who didn't even deserve it—a dented can.

In your early stages of recovery, if you meet someone you know has the potential to be the one, you must first and foremost let them know your situation. Honesty is key. If she is truly interested in you, you being in recovery wouldn't be a deal breaker. It would grant you more respect from her for the simple fact that you started the relationship with pure honesty, which would make her feel more inclined to motivate and help you through your recovery, go to meetings with you, and be aware of enabling or triggering you. It would be like building a relationship on a foundation of honesty, and by six months, you will both fully understand each other.

So, my time in recovery for a relationship is six months. For a friendship, you might meet her in six days. There are a few more issues I have with A.A./N.A. that I will discuss in a later chapter, but one thing I now highly agree on is that two people in recovery should not be in a relationship. Here's the problem: women in early recovery, as well as men, don't know how to just enjoy things sometimes without getting feelings involved. It's like a golden rule in Falmouth: "If we have sex, then we are together." So if I met you at a meeting on Thursday, then on Saturday we meet up, hang out, and end up having sex, that automatically makes us boyfriend and girlfriend? Men are the worst. It's like we are more vulnerable when we don't have a substance to protect us from feelings. A female can have sex with you because she's sexually attracted to you. However, that doesn't mean she wants a full-blown relationship. I've seen so many fallouts in meetings and recovery functions over two girls having sex with the same guy, or two guys having sex with the same girl. The conclusion is always the same: the parties involved misinterpret the difference between being in a relationship and just having a good time.

This leads me to my last piece of advice given to me by Momma Martha: Never get into a relationship with someone in recovery—it never works out. You know why? Because "Two crumbs don't make a cookie."

Chapter 10

The last chapter serves as a perfect introduction to what I'm about to explain regarding the end result of my downfall, which led me to spend another year in prison.

Before I go further, I would like to reiterate a statement I made earlier in this book. Some things just happen for a reason. Causes bring effects, and there is no such thing as coincidence. So, with that being said, if none of this would have happened, one, I would have never seen my brother again; two, I would have probably still been running around, drinking and acting like a fool, which would have led to God knows what; and last, my plans would have never manifested, which would have ultimately resulted in me never writing this book. So, I now look at it as a blessing in disguise.

Earlier, I left you with Becky being apprehended in New York by her mom and placed in a mental health hospital for evaluation. At this point, I'm down and out bad. I lost my job, I got kicked out of the sober home, and my support system, which was Becky, is no longer around. So now I'm wallowing in my own shit. I had it all, and just like that, I lost everything. I was too embarrassed to go back home. Mind you, all of this is going on and my probation officer doesn't know shit, even though I know she is going to eventually find out. So, I made the smartest decision possible, and I called her. "Hey James," I say. "Hi Jessica, I have an issue." She asks, "What's wrong?" I tell her, "I relapsed, and I'm so humiliated." She then says, "Okay James, where are you right now?" I tell her, "I'm in a hotel right now trying to figure out what to do." I lied; I was at my nephew's house in Boston, but I knew she would have flipped out because she didn't want me there. She then tells me that I needed to get back into detoxes, and I need to call around for a bed and let her know when I found one. So, I called Gosnold again and I did the intake. Two days later, they called me and told me that I had a spot. I called my P.O. immediately and told her. She says, "great." The same day I got to the detox, I got called to the front entrance for a visitor, which was odd. It was my P.O. She was checking to see if I was lying.

That was the vegetables of this debacle; now it's time for the meat and potatoes. Remember, every time—and I mean every time—I check into a detox, I leave with a female, and this time was no different. As per usual, when I first came in, I took my alpha-male stroll through the building to let my presence be known. Looking at the pickings, there were a few decent ones, but nothing to write home about. Until I walked into the dining room and I saw this dark-skinned, gorgeous young woman sitting there. She had beautiful skin, natural African hair, and was well kept. So I could easily tell through my experience in recovery that she was in detox for alcohol.

Anyhow, to speed things up a bit, I chose her to be my sidekick. We spent the whole detox with each other, and we stuck together like white on rice. When it was discharging time, we both left together. Now, at this point, we knew little of each other but knew enough to know we wanted one another. So, the day we left, which was the Fourth of July, we went to my favorite place, the **Admiralty Inn**, and got a room for two days. It's the fourth, so you know what's going on: partying, partying, and more partying. We both relapsed the same day we got out of detox… smh.

After spending the weekend together, we ended up going back to Boston. She lived in a town over from me called **Lynn**. We continued seeing each other and continued with our toxic affair for two weeks. She spoiled me and basically filled the void of Becky. To be honest, we really kind of liked each other. She said I was the male version of her, and she was the female version of me. Now that I think of it, she was right… two crumbs.

One early morning, I get a FaceTime call from her, it's like 8 a.m. She's looking sad and tells me we need to talk, and she wants to come to see me ASAP. I said, "OK." When she pulled up, I hopped into the car, and she looked wicked depressed and started crying. I asked, "What's wrong? Why are you so sad?" She said, "James, I feel like I'm losing control over my life." This is when I learned that in life, shit may look good, but it's not always what it seems. I looked at her like she was bugging. I say, "S, you don't even drink like that. When you're with me, you drink socially, so what's really going on?" She said, "James, we didn't even give ourselves a chance. I went to detox so I can get clean. It's like I did that for nothing." Now I'm feeling guilty because although we both mutually agreed to drink that day, I could've been the man and said no. So now I'm thinking to myself, okay, so where do we go from here? She answered it for me. She said, "James, I am about to do intake. I'm going back to detox, and this time I'm giving myself a chance." Honestly, at this point, I'm all the way back on the streets. My plan at this point is to get a bunch of drugs from my connect and accumulate a lot of cash because I haven't spoken to my P.O. since detox. So, I know there is a great chance I'm getting booked. I tell her, "Listen, I totally understand. You have my full support on this decision. Let's just chill until they call you for the bed, and while you're in there, make sure you call me every day to let me know if you need anything. I'm here for you." She says, "What? No, I don't think you understand." I say, "Why?" She says, "James, your life is a disaster now, look at you. You were doing so good on the Cape, now you're back to doing the same shit you just did all that time in prison. I came here so we both can do intake, your drinking is out of control." I'm in full-blown denial as it is now 9 a.m. and I've got two nips in my pocket, and just downed one before she pulled up, straight tripping. I then say to her, "Listen, S, I'm not trying to do that detox and treatment shit again, I'm cool. You just go and I got you." She gives me the ultimate threat, "James, if you don't come with me, when I pull out of this parking lot this will be the last time you ever see me." That moment I learned the true meaning of finding love in a hopeless place. We met at a detox, and we fell in drunk love with each other. I couldn't refuse her. Besides, maybe this would keep me from not going back to jail.

We both do intake over the phone, and twenty minutes later they call her back with a bed space. She has private insurance. There's no bed space for me yet. I tell her, "I tried, baby, don't worry, just go and do what you gotta do, I'll be here." She's like, "No." I'm like, "What do you mean, no?" She says, "You know eventually they are going to call you." I said, "OK, then when they call, I'll come" … lying. She says, "No, you're going to come with me to the detox and wait in the car in the parking lot until they call you to come in." I'm like, "Are you serious?" She's dead serious.

Speeding things up, we are now back in **Falmouth**. It's three hours before it's time for her to check in, and I still haven't got a phone call yet. We check into my favorite place again to have some fun before it's time. We're drinking, eating, and just savoring the last moments of inebriation before it's time to give it all up again. Now, I forgot to tell you, as I said while I was back in Boston, I had got me a little "package" and started hustling again, and instead of leaving the shit, I brought it with me to Falmouth. So now it's time for her to check in. We pulled up to the detox, she kisses me and tells me she'll see me soon. Before going forward, it's important that I tell you that on our way there, I spoke to S and told her, "Listen, don't switch up on me. I'm doing this because it's what's best for us, don't sell me out." Moving on, she goes in. I'm sitting in the car, relaxing. Then suddenly, 15 minutes later, S comes out with a recovery assistant. Of course, I know her. She says, "Hey James, how are you?" I say, "Fine. And yourself?" She says, "Oh, I'm great." She then says, "Well, unfortunately, we don't have a bed for you right now." I say, "I know, I'm cool though," thinking she knows what's up. Suddenly, S says, "James, give me the keys to the car, I can't trust you in it." I said, "Excuse me?" She says, "Yeah, I need my keys." I say, "OK," and give the keys to her. They walk off, but I'm still in the car. Three minutes later I get a text from her saying, "I'm sorry." Now I'm confused. Next thing you know, the RA pops up again. She says, "Hey James, unfortunately, we don't have a bed so you're going to have to leave the property until we do." Now I'm steaming mad, and the alcohol is starting to affect my judgment. I told her to get S for me; she said no. They're not allowing her to come out of the building. Now I snap. I came all the way back out here with this girl, and not only does she sell me out, but she also abandoned me. Now I'm way out here stranded. I blew a gasket and went crazy out in the parking lot.

While this was happening, they notified Martha, and she called one of my recovery brothers. He called me and bought me a Lyft to take me to the hotel and meet me there. I told him what happened, and he was livid. Come to find out, he also relapsed and was already scheduled for a bed, and I did intake before him. Why? Because they won't take me in the detox until S leaves. Now I'm wondering what the hell did she say to these people? Now the plan is I must admit into Falmouth Hospital until a bed is ready for me at the detox, so that's what I did. I took a nap, then decided that I wanted to go out and smoke a cigarette. Unbeknownst to me, I'm not allowed to go smoke a cigarette because I'm not allowed to leave the building. So, I riffed about it.

Out of nowhere, I see two officers come in. But I paid them no mind, because to my knowledge, I didn't do anything wrong. They walked up to me and said, "What's the problem?" I say, "Man, nothing, I'm going out to smoke a cigarette." Suddenly, he grabbed me and threw the cuffs on me! I'm asking him, "What the hell are you arresting me for?" He said, "Protective custody." I say, "Man, I'm here voluntarily!" He ignored me, then started searching me… this is where my luck ran out… in my lighter pocket, I had a bag of crack rocks on me. Due to me being a fucking drunk, I had totally forgot about it. Before he found it on me, which was inevitable, I told the officer that I get high, which was a lie, and that I had drugs on me. They charged me with distribution, which later got dropped to a simple possession. That night I had also found out that my P.O. put a warrant out for my arrest.

I now have the courage today to say that I've never been suicidal; I always stood up like a man and faced my adversities. But that night, I felt like I had had enough. To the point, I had asked the cop to do me a favor. He said, "What's that?" I told him, "Take me around the back and blow my head off." He said, "Hell no, kid, it ain't that serious." I said, "Man, only if you knew, I've just completely lost everything I've worked hard to accomplish… it's all over." He ignored me and put me in the cell with a big gulp and a sub from Seven Eleven.

Six months later, while I was incarcerated, I heard from S. And from what she told me, the shit that Gosnold told her about me scared and manipulated her to do what she had done to me. Why? I have no clue. I've never said, nor have I ever done anything to disrespect them. So why would they want to destroy my character, or furthermore, make me out to look like a villain? Questions that deserve answers in later days.

Chapter 11

Earlier in the book, I mentioned how many of my resources and tools I've used on my road to recovery come from the literature of PhDs and people considered veterans. I have a belief that if you haven't been sober for at least two years, yes, we can help each other, but as far as you teaching me recovery, I'd rather learn from a vet.

The Big Book to me is not as helpful as the alternatives I've used as references in this book. My favorite, though, is Allen Berger, Ph.D. His self-help books put recovery in a simpler, and more down-to-earth process for me. It also took away the feeling of me belonging to a cult, a feeling I got when I was an adamant member of A.A. In Twelve Stupid Things That Mess Up Recovery, Allen states that "Those who do best in recovery are those who are honest with themselves, open to new ideas and experiences, and willing to take direction." In this book, Allen gives us 12 issues that mess up recovery, but I'm going to focus on three of them to further explain my main problems with the A.A./N.A. program.

BELIEVING SOBRIETY WILL FIX EVERYTHING

Just because you are sober doesn't mean all of your problems go away. You may think clearly and come up with sound solutions to deal with your problems, but it takes self-help work to solve the problems you were drowning in a substance.

My mental health state, stemming from my long period of incarceration and dealing with the death of my family, led me to drink more to drown the pain away. Once the substance was gone, however, the pain got stronger. I had to figure out ways to cope with my mental health without relying on a substance. At first, I substituted alcohol with psych meds until I realized I was just drowning my issues away with another substance. So, I figured out better addictions that will not only keep me from running to a bottle but will also help me live a healthier life, such as exercise, cooking, and going shopping—anything that will take my mind off the cravings. To deal with my anxiety, sex also played a big part in my short seven-month length of sobriety. Whenever I felt the urge to relapse, I would either have sex or masturbate. It usually helped just enough for the urges to go away.

Some people rely on meetings to keep them grounded. I used to until I realized that meetings were just another crutch. Some people are addicted to meetings just as much as they are to a substance. They believe that if they miss a meeting, it will increase the risk of them relapsing. I believe that's just psychological. Meetings are helpful at times. You've got shit on your mind you'd like to share and get feedback from members. It's good to go where you feel comfortable getting things off your chest. But that is also what a sponsor is for. When you go day to day, thinking rationally, without the crutches of meetings or living in a sober home, and get through without relapsing… every day… you're winning… one day at a time.

BEING SELECTIVELY HONEST.

This is a big beef I have with the program. Before I go forward, Allen Berger is an adamant A.A. supporter, and although I take a lot of value out of what he teaches, there are times when I don't agree with him as well.

When it comes to A.A., I adopt the 12 steps of recovery and compare them to the Ten Commandments. If you follow the Ten Commandments, you pretty much live a righteous life. If you follow the 12 steps of recovery, you are living a grateful, honest life of sobriety. But just like the Bible, the Big Book can also be interpreted in different ways, especially when it comes to what's accepted as being the honest truth.

Basically, in my belief, the Big Book is the holy bible of a cult called A.A., and A.A. is the platform being used to justify the belief system that fuels the major agenda of the big business of recovery. If you go against anything the A.A. community believes… you are the devil.

Now stick with me, because I'm about to tell you some shit that is probably going to make some people mad at me, but the truth is the truth.

For opioid addicts, they have this program called M.A.T., or Medical Assisted Treatment. In this program, in order to help you kick your opioid addiction and maintain your recovery, they prescribe you maintenance medication, which is either Suboxone or Methadone. Synthetic dopamine to help you "block" the craving of opioids. However, when taken they give you the same feeling as if you were on opioids. Many people that are in recovery are in the maintenance program.

With alcohol recovery, there really isn't a maintenance program besides two injection options: Vivitrol or Antabuse. Both will make you violently ill if you drink on them, deterring you from wanting a drink at all. And the side effects are questionable, like erectile dysfunction. Meaning it's a possibility that if you take one of those shots, you can end up with a permanent noodle... hell naw, lol.

Now this is my first gripe: addiction is addiction, no matter if it's alcohol or opioids. But I believe if your primary addiction of choice is alcohol, you belong to Alcoholics Anonymous. If your addiction is primarily narcotics, you belong to Narcotics Anonymous. Perfect example, I'm a drunk. Me going to an N.A. meeting is pointless because I don't have N.A. issues. The only time I go to N.A. meetings is to either scope out chicks, or if one of my fellow recovery brothers asked me to accompany them. Even then, I feel guilty because there was a time I was a part of their problems. So, I would feel like the wolf in sheep's clothing.

However, there are people who go to A.A. meetings whose choice of poison was never alcohol. Yeah, they might have indulged in it from time to time, but their number one choice of drug was opioids, and a lot of them are on maintenance drugs. Meaning, although they're not using opioids, they're still using a man-made substance that acts and gives the same pleasure as an opioid. Therefore, making them cheaters... yeah, I said it... YOU'RE A CHEATER!

The reason why the "cheaters" go to A.A. is that, although they are sober from alcohol, which really wasn't their substance of choice anyway, if they don't drink, they are still considered sober because maintenance drugs are accepted in the world of recovery. So, although they're nodding off from a strip of Suboxone in the middle of a meeting, their recovery is still intact.

That's why alcoholics have the worst addiction because there is no maintenance for it. So, relapses are more common. N.A. members who are going through recovery without M.A.T. are placed on a higher pedestal than those who are, which explains why opioid abusers in recovery who use M.A.T. would rather go to A.A. meetings where they feel more comfortable in their own skin. Because in the N.A. community they are judged. To the ones who white-knuckled it through without the help of synthetic dope… they are considered frauds.

Another fucked up point, which is fueled by the N.A./A.A. belief system but utilized by the big businessmen of recovery, is what mental health deems acceptable to be used for mental health drugs. In my state, and in about 60 percent of America, marijuana has been recognized as a medically cleared mental health drug. It has been proven to be helpful with anxiety, depression, and significant chronic illnesses. Your therapist or psych doctor can actually make you a medical patient and prescribe you marijuana with a registration card to verify it.

However, substance abuse and mental health treatment centers refuse to recognize marijuana as a mental health or M.A.T. prescribed drug. In fact, whenever you bring the topic up in a group they silence you or change the subject, using marijuana being a "gateway drug" as a justification, when it's already been documented that there is no real evidence for that claim.

It's always business, nothing personal. Think about all the money drug companies would lose if they allowed treatment centers to be pro-marijuana. You have at least 100 different types of mental health drugs being prescribed daily. Weed is natural, you can grow it. Why would I pay the drug company for something I can grow on my own? Or buy for way cheaper at a dispensary?

Weed can also be used as a M.A.T., but they won't allow that because the cult of recovery is highly against it, although they have no problem with you sticking synthetic dope underneath your tongue. For the record, some say coming off Suboxone or Methadone is worse than coming off the actual drug itself, to the point it becomes a habit. Most heroin addicts in recovery who relapse, one of the main reasons why? They run out of maintenance meds or get cut off from them entirely. Facts.

FEELING SPECIAL OR UNIQUE

Another disagreement. You are supposed to feel special and unique, because you are. The creator made all of us to be different in our own unique way. However, being special and unique doesn't mean I'm better or worse than anybody. It doesn't give me the right to judge.

In A.A. communities, it kills me when individuals who have a decent amount of sobriety time under their belt tend to believe that gives them the right to judge or criticize others. We call them "big book thumpers." The ones that try so hard to show that the program is working for them, to the point they start to look phony.

If you have two or less years of recovery under your belt, you are still considered to be in early recovery. I was only able to make it to seven months. But during those seven months, I felt the difference, physically and mentally. I loved it, but I also humbled myself and remained down to earth to the ones who were fresh in the program. I tried to make them feel as comfortable as possible and furthermore let them know that we are all in the same battle. I'm no better or no worse. Always be grateful for every day you go without a drink or a drug, because one day you can be straight, then the next you can slip. Nobody's perfect. 70 percent of people in recovery go through the spin cycle multiple times before they finally get it. A lot of people, it took years for them to become part of the thirty percent. Some had to lose everything, loved ones included.

When you have years of sobriety over people, it doesn't make you smarter or a more prestigious person in the program. It doesn't mean you have immunity to judge the ones that slip. Many people such as I are new to dealing with humility. When I slipped, I didn't even want to go to meetings out of fear of embarrassment, humiliation, and self-defeat. To go from recently receiving my 7-month chip to now having to go up for a twenty-four? Want to talk about shame? That was probably the most humiliating day of my life. But what hurts me the most is when guys who you thought were your friends act like they care about you bouncing back from your slip-up. But behind your back, they're kicking your name in the dirt. "Oh, we knew he was going to fuck up, it was only a matter of time." Straight praying and waiting for my downfall. I respect men. I respect men that'll say straight in your face what's really on their mind. I can't stand back-biters. I'm talking so much of a creep that they're not even aware that you know they're slandering you. The ones that are genuinely rooting for your comeback are the ones that's telling you what's being said about you.

The fucked-up thing about it all is that I still respect these dudes because I know they don't know no better. They used to be the biggest crackheads in the state and had to lose it all to finally say it was time to change. Now they have multiple years of sobriety under their belt, great jobs, and good women in their life. They are focused on their recovery and attend meetings adamantly.

I just want the ones who took the time to read my book to know that I'm far from a hater. I will cherish the day that I'm able to go up and receive my one-year chip, let alone the day I'm able to say that I have multiple years of sobriety. So, I applaud them. With the willingness of my creator, I will get there one day. But to the ones who know who they are, although you kicked my back in, I know you all still have enough respect for me to read my book. I'm not going to put you out there, but when I see you, just make amends, because I know you was talking shit!

Chapter 12

In the book When A.A. Doesn't Work for You: Rational Steps to Quitting Alcohol by Albert Ellis, Ph.D., and Emmit Velten, Ph.D., the method they teach to reach and maintain sobriety, known as rational emotive therapy or R.E.T., gave me a better sense of how to decrease my chances of relapsing by simply working on changing the way I ultimately think.

The ABC formula: A + B = C. A is for the activating events in your life that trigger your addiction, plus B, the belief of what you tell yourself about the activating event, which adds up to C, the consequence, or the actual decision of you choosing to either relapse or avoid it.

For example: in my situation, after work I liked to go out and hang with long-time friends who are not in recovery. In an environment which consists of alcohol (Activating Event), I, knowing I have a problem with drinking, start to think irrationally. My irrational thinking tells me, "I work hard, I'm not getting in trouble with the law, and I'm being a productive member of society. Fuck it, I deserve to drink and enjoy myself with my boys" (Irrational Belief). So I end up drinking and throw my sobriety out the window (Consequence).

Now that I've switched my B's from irrational to rational, it more so goes like this: me knowing that my homeboys are not seeking sobriety like I am, if I choose to go and hang out, I know there is a possibility I might be triggered by all the alcohol that will be provided at this function (Activating Event). Me knowing that when I drink, I don't know how to stop, and right now things are going great for me. Although I would have fun tonight, I know in the long run it will come back to haunt me (Rational Belief). Fuck it, I'll see them another time in a less triggering environment. They might look at me differently, but I know what's best for me. Either they can accept it or leave me alone. So I stayed home (Consequence).

By switching up the way I think about drinking and the consequences of it, I learned to help myself by practicing to be honest with how I react when I think irrationally, instead of logically, for the purpose of psyching myself into believing I can control my problem, when in fact I know that I'm powerless over it. Instead of just thinking if you surrender and leave it in your creator's hands, without making any effort to help yourself, you can work on having acceptance and honesty in the way that your belief system dictates a better choice of action.

Another example: during my 90-month sentence in federal prison, I learned what arguably can be considered the worst business or trade I possibly could have, although some of you might beg to differ. Anyway, I learned to take sugar, potatoes, and oranges, put it all together, and let it sit for seven days to make hooch… jailhouse wine. To take it further, I also mastered the art of burning the wine with a homemade heating device, which turns it into two hundred proof pure alcohol. Simply put, imagine if a monkey knew how to grow bananas? Exactly. I learned how to create the same poison that was destroying me. Satan had cursed me with a gift. I used to make gallons of wine. To make matters worse, I worked in food service so all the ingredients I needed, I used to steal from the kitchen. Although I survived manufacturing alcohol, I also indulged every day. There were times I wanted to slow down, but couldn't because I was the one making it. Like if a heroin addict knew how to manufacture his own heroin, how hard would it be to quit?

When I went back to prison to serve my one-year sentence, I had plenty of opportunities to start another alcohol enterprise. People who knew me were begging to invest in me, and the money is pretty good. However, me being on a different path, staying honest with myself, and accepting my disease, I use my rational thinking to change my belief system about making wine. First off, my time there was way too short for me to focus on any jailhouse business. For two, I had more important things to occupy my time with, such as writing this book. And finally, I was in recovery, and by the time I was getting out, I had a year of sobriety under my belt. Me knowing me, and being honest with myself, I know if I had begun to make wine, eventually I would've indulged, which furthermore would've contradicted my reasons for writing this book. I would be a fraud. That rational belief about my activating event—manufacturing and distributing alcohol—led me to the consequences I stand at today: writing this book with the gratitude to say that I am still sober, still accepting my honest self, and proud to be in recovery for another day, one day at a time.

For the record, I have the utmost respect for those who chose the A.A. program as their culture and follow the Big Book. Although it didn't work for me, I never said it didn't work at all. What I did like about A.A. is that it held you accountable for the choices you made. A lot of people choose self-help over A.A. because they don't like answering to others. In A.A., whether it's your sponsor, the group you belong to, or the house manager that runs your sober home, you have someone to answer to. Most people need that kind of structure through the first year of recovery, until they feel comfortable enough to live in the world on their own without an authoritative figure keeping them in line.

Plus, I love the community. Everyone is on the same boat, battling addiction, working on bettering themselves. At the same time, you build a camaraderie. I have recovery brothers that I was blessed to meet because I went through the program. I respect these dudes for the fact that their love was unconditional. I can call them right now as I'm writing this sentence, and they will be there for me.

I'll end by saying this, though: it's one thing to utilize the structure of the program to start you off and gradually work your way to self-sufficiency. It's another thing to be so scared of relapsing that you basically make yourself content with living in a structured environment forever. Never be too dependent on the program. Sober homes were meant to be temporary, not forever. You can't be scared to live in the world. The only way you can reach true recovery is if you can live on your own, stay sober, and not let the urges of the world bother you, characteristics I believe you're more likely to claim through self-help and rational emotive thinking.

Chapter 13

I must admit, I'm a very vindictive person when it comes to me feeling used or humiliated, especially when I'm in a position where I can't control the situation or the outcome, like for instance, with women. It took me some time to promptly admit when I was wrong, and sometimes, like now, I find myself in denial.

When you commit crimes, you must understand the odds of you going to jail are high. And the chances of you losing people and things are inevitable. At first, when you look at things from a selfish point of view, and when people decide to move on with their lives, you feel betrayed or left for dead. Especially when it's people you were looking out for and were around you for the good times but wouldn't stick around for the bad ones. It hurts, trust me, I've been through it. I'm going through it now as we speak. But this time around, I accepted the fact that me making the choices to break the law and not follow the rules resulted in the consequences I had to deal with. And furthermore, it played a big part in people going on with their lives without me. Life doesn't pause because you're in prison. Sometimes you are blessed with people that will be there for you in a time of need, but to expect them to pause life because of you is outright selfish.

Which brings me to a fucked-up decision I made where I let my feelings get the best of me. Mind you, I made a few when I was doing my one-year sentence, feeling like if a motherfucker leaves you during a one-year sentence, they are just some unloyal pieces of shit. But the first, and most selfish shit, I let my feelings lead me to write Becky one of the most disrespectful emails you can think of.

Becky ended up moving to Florida after she was released from the hospital stemming from the New York incident. During this time, I found myself back behind bars for one year. Now, mind you, when I went back,

I finally got back in contact with Becky. She was looking out for me substantially—money, phone calls, and emails—despite her mom's wishes for her to leave me alone. Becky was basically all I had to make my time go smoothly, and she did. What I failed to remember is that Becky is in the world, she is not 100 percent mentally, and all it's going to take is for someone to realize how mentally challenged she is, and how much money she's worth, to dedicate his effort to capturing her for himself and furthermore manipulating her to leave me alone.

Well, it basically happened. One day I call her and she says, "James, I have something to tell you." I say, "Oh God, go ahead." She says, "I've been dealing with this guy. He's very hot and I really like him." I say, "Really, okay" (lol). She then says, "James, I love you but I don't think it's right to love two people." I say, "OK" (lol). Then she says, "I don't think me and you can talk anymore." I say to her, "Wow, but we are just friends, wtf?" She says, "I know, but I realized I can't just be your friend because I love you too much and it's not right to him." I asked her, "Becky, when did you meet this dude?" She says, "a week ago." A week ago? WTF!? I say to her, "Becky, listen, fuck the love, and understand that I'm talking to you as a friend, or more so a brother. It's one thing to like someone that you just met a week ago, but to sit here and say you love him, and basically tell me that you can no longer speak to me or be friends with me because of it, does that sound normal to you?" She says, "Yes, now please respect my wishes," and hangs up on me. I'm steaming mad.

Now, is this the first time she has done this? No. But to say she's leaving me for dead for someone else? Definitely a first. We had made a pact: no matter what position we are in, we will always remain friends. But me going through Becky's episodes with bipolar so many times, I also know that Becky will say one thing on Monday, then say another on Tuesday, then on Wednesday, apologize for what she said on Monday. For some reason, however, this day, I didn't consider any of that when I decided to write her an email that went like this...

Becky, You are the dumbest, retarded honkey I've ever met in my life. You are 30 yrs old, with a 12-yr-old brain. To have trusted you is a testimony to how much of an idiot I must be. If they had to put a face by the definition of imbecile, you would be the mascot. Once any man finds out how slow you are, he's just going to fuck you, spend all your money, then leave you. That's why your mom runs all your boyfriends away to protect you. Because she knows you are not mentally capable of protecting yourself. I cared about you genuinely, regardless of the challenges that come with you. I accepted the fact of us being friends, but it seems like every time a man sticks his dick in your ass, you forget where your loyalty lies. So, with that being said, fuck you, and thanks for showing me how much of a piece of shit you are. I hope when he breaks your heart… you end up back in a psych ward.

Pretty fucked up, right? I know. That night I lay in my cell under my covers, feeling bad. I knew how hurtful it was going to be when she read that email. Becky didn't do anything to me. All she did was decide to live her life. But me being selfish only thinking of myself and my feelings, I didn't consider what Becky was going through. If I had sat and thought rationally about the situation, I would've handled it in a different fashion. I knew Becky didn't think situations all the way through before she made choices. I knew this because there were times when I was physically there and had to literally counsel her through common-sense shit. What if she runs into someone that is the opposite of me? With different motives? To me, when I met Becky in that Zoom meeting, I didn't know she was rich until later. I naturally liked her personality and her character. She could've lived in a cardboard box; it wouldn't have changed anything.

I was Becky's protector. She was coming to me for protection, yet instead, I verbally abused her, letting my stinking thinking get the best of me. I felt so bad. I know Becky didn't mean to hang up, she just didn't know what else to do or say. She was so used to me coming to the rescue and taking over the matter, helping her use her rational thinking instead of just moving on impulse. When I spazzed out on her, she was confused.

What I did next made me realize how much I've grown to accept humility and face it with honesty. Life doesn't revolve around you. You must consider others, especially if you care about them. I emailed her an apology and some words of wisdom. It went like this…

Becky, I want to take this time to deeply apologize for my last email. That was totally uncalled for and highly disrespectful and I'm so humiliated and embarrassed for acting like a little kid. I just want you to know that I wish nothing but the best for you, and I pray that you find it in your heart to forgive me for those harsh words. I know you can be special if someone gives you the courage and the motivation to beat your mental illness. I just don't want anyone to take advantage of you. My relationship with you goes beyond intimacy, beyond money, I care about you for who you are, and it's an honor to be your friend, and your protector. You are special, Becky, always remember that. Even if you decide to never speak to me again, please remember that Becky, you are special, and you deserve the best. Don't let anyone ever tell you differently. Till next time… praying that there is a next time… take care.

Fortunately, Becky responded to my email. She accepted my apology, and I respected her position. We are friends, and she said that will never change. She said she was just going through a down point when she said what she said, and she must start being mindful that certain things can be hurtful. What's crazy is this though, she said when she read the word "honkey" she started laughing. I know some of you good ol' white folk didn't find anything humorous at all about it… I also know in your younger days when you got mad at a Black person, we were all kinds of niggers and monkeys. So suck it up, because I had to for years… shit. Don't get all sensitive now (lol).

Jojo, that's what I'm going to call her, because if I use her name she will sue the shit out of me. Me and Jojo's situation is a little more complicated. I have known Jojo since we were kids. We were raised in the same neighborhood. She is a Haitian and comes from a very boujee background. Jojo used to look at us project kids like we were beneath her.

She would never speak to us, let alone date us. Her brother Petey was my boy though.

Like any other overseas family living in the hood however, Jojo's mom got her money right and moved out of the projects. I brought her up because as I continue to take inventory of myself, I've come to accept that when I'm in love with someone, and I feel like they betrayed me, once I turn off, it's hard for me to turn completely back on. To the point I get very inconsiderate of the other person's feelings. I can still love you but have hidden resentment towards you.

Anyway, Jojo was pretty. But what stuck out to me the most about her was her voluptuousness. Jojo was so thick in the right place, it was like the creator made her with a chisel. Out of all my boys in the projects, I was the one to win her heart. I was in love with Jojo. She was a good woman. She cooked well and was very clean. The only thing wrong was she didn't like how I chose to live my life, which is understandable. She always used to try and talk me out of being in the streets, but I wouldn't pay it no mind. She was the type of person that'll criticize what you do but would have no problem reaping the benefits. Two months go by, and we're in love… or so I thought… she disappears.

She won't answer my calls; I go by her house and she's never there… I'm like, damn. A month later, she pops up out of nowhere telling me she's pregnant by another dude. So I started to do the math in my head. It's only been a month since I've seen you, so if you're pregnant, that means you were dealing with someone else behind my back!?... wow.

Anyway, speeding this up… I go to jail. I do my fed bid. Seven and a half years later I get a Facebook request from a Denise… it's Jojo. I accepted, we linked up, and everything was cool. At the time she is in a relationship, and so am I, but we're still fornicating on a regular basis. I met the boys. Notice I said boys. She had twins. They were 9 years old. When I see them, I started to feel resentment because in my head I'm thinking, "Damn, these little dudes are supposed to be mine." But I had always kept that thought to myself.

Overall, when I had went to the Cape, Jojo was still around for the most part and had wanted to leave her boyfriend to start a relationship with me, but I wouldn't commit. Before I left for the Cape, I asked Jojo to be with me, and she said no. Now that I'm getting my shit together, you feel as though you can just come in and out of my life as you please. I was being stubborn, and I must admit… very resentful. She was a good woman, I just wasn't willing to change, and she didn't want to live with always having to worry about me. But when she noticed the difference between me being in Boston, to me being in the Cape, she was willing to be with me. I live now by that saying, if you are not with me while I'm down, keep that same energy when I'm up. What's crazy is this though, the last time I had seen Jojo, she came to visit me in the Cape, and we had sex… the last time I've heard from her she sent me a text of a sonogram telling me to say hi to my son. I haven't heard from her or seen her since.

In both situations, I was wrong. In both situations, I had to use rational thinking to admit that I was wrong. Going through heartbreak and struggling to accept your role in the negative outcomes in your life are all parts of the growth process in recovery. Kicking a substance is just the beginning. Solving your activating events by changing your beliefs leads to better consequences, which is longevity in recovery… and your sanity.

Chapter 14

In the book, "12 Stupid Things That Mess Up Recovery", Berger states: "The twelve steps are a powerful program of change. They evoke a multitude of healing forces that can save life and open doors we would have never thought possible." When I started my step work and began dissecting myself morally and truthfully, a lot of ideas started to pop up in my head, like effortlessly. It's like when you harness the positive energy inside of you, it triggers positive thoughts, which lead to positive ideas. The same goes for negative energy. Napoleon Hill in "Think and Grow Rich" states a prophetic line written by English poet W.C. Henley: "I am a master of my fate; I am the captain of my soul." Napoleon states that what makes this line breathe is the fact that our creator gave us the power to control our thoughts. He states that this power makes no attempt to discriminate between constructive and destructive thoughts. To reiterate one last piece of this literature to further justify my beliefs going forward, he states that "Our brains become magnetized with dominating thoughts we hold in our minds, by means which no one is familiar. These magnets attract to us the forces, the people, and the circumstances of life which harmonize with the nature of our dominating thoughts."

My point is, if you think it enough, and have the faith and desire to make your thoughts materialize… it will happen. In my past life of crime, I had found it somewhat amazing how when I set my mind to believing I can do illegal activities, I would achieve my objectives. For example, one year my mom was backed up on money and it was Christmas time. At this time, my daughter was 4 years old, and my niece and nephew were also young. Grandma was living her last days; we basically knew that this would be her final holiday with us. I had thought to myself, "I gotta step up and make this Christmas memorable," so with determination and desire… I was destined to make a couple of grand to make sure the kids had a decent Christmas. Although I knew I was taking a high risk of going to jail… I didn't care… I was determined. When the kids woke up for Christmas and seen all that shit under the tree, it made me feel good. To be looked at as a man from my grandmother's eyes before she passed, and to see the relief on my momma's face.

But the reality of it is that I let negative energy fuel my negative thoughts to manifest negative ideas, which ultimately ended in a negative outcome. I had committed suicide. To make one day possible, I spent 185 days in jail. Before I began my journey of recovery, I had felt that it was worth it. But now me being completely honest with myself, I know my daughter, niece, and my nephew would've preferred me to be around for those 185 days, rather than enjoy one day of playing with toys.

I am now in the process of learning how to completely control the power of my thoughts. To be able to harness the positive energy that I need to create positive ideas that will make me a successful and honorable member of society. When I analyze my rational beliefs, I concluded that when I process legitimate ideas in my head, not only does it come so easy to me, the logistics of the process and the execution of these ideas become so convenient, it's like I was meant to materialize it.

To interpret in a simpler way, when I was forced to sit my ass down and realize that I will never prosper from doing fucked up shit, I let the power of my thoughts gravitate from destructive to constructive thinking. Then I came up with the idea to write this book. My desire now is to reach out to the ones who come from the same type of environment as me, regardless of what part of this country you are from. To let them know that it's okay to be real with yourself and face your realities. Our minds were trained for many years by outside forces, who designed society to make us believe that drinking, selling drugs, using drugs, robbing, stealing, killing, and repping street signs and colors is all a part of our culture, and that is how we are supposed to live. Not only do I want to nurture my people, I also want to lead by example. I want to be the proof that changing your way of thinking and altering your belief in a more rational and positive direction, even a federal convict from the ghetto can become an inspiration. You don't have to be a rapper, or an athlete to make it out. There are so many opportunities if we just learn how to think outside of the box.

In "Think and Grow Rich," Napoleon Hill states, "Every human being that understands the purpose of money wishes for it. Wishing will not bring riches. But desiring riches with a state of mind that becomes an obsession, then planning definite ways and means to acquire riches, and backing those plans with persistence that does not recognize failure… will bring riches."

I advise anyone who is chasing happiness and wealth to read "Think and Grow Rich" by Napoleon Hill. But just don't read the book—study it and follow the directions. Let that shit marinate in your head. That book is like the Holy Bible to me. Learn the 6 steps. I'm not going to state them, but if you truly want to know them, you will read the book. I can lead you to water, but I can't force you to drink it.

I am 40 years old. By the age of 43, I want to be known for my book nationwide. I want to run two sober homes. I want to be worth six figures by my 43rd birthday, which is September 27th, 2027. In return, I plan to give the knowledge and wisdom I obtained from living the steps to the youth, and to the ones with the desire to change. My plans start with this book.

I say this statement to myself twice a day. I let it manifest in my head to the point it becomes a definite. I will achieve this goal because I am obsessed with the desire to do so. And my faith is so certain on it, nothing and no one is going to stop me.

Chapter 15

Step 11: Sought through prayer and meditation to improve our conscious contact with God as we understood him, praying only for knowledge of his will for us and the power to carry it out.

When do you know you've reached the point to safely say that you are fully recovered? Is it even possible to reach the stage in life when you can say, "I've accomplished everything life has to offer," or "I am fully restored with my sanity and have reached complete recovery?" I know people who have thirty-plus years of sobriety under their belts and still go to meetings, introduce themselves as alcoholics or addicts, and say they are still in recovery. My recovery brother, Scott D, has been sober for multiple years now. He doesn't go to meetings and he hasn't done his step work. As a matter of fact, he hates the big book so much, the first time I met him he literally lit it on fire! He says it's all a crock of bullshit. Yet, how does he manage to stay sober? He "white knuckles" it, meaning, although he doesn't participate in the recovery community, he mingles with A.A./N.A. members, and he works in recovery to keep himself surrounded by people in recovery. He magnetizes the energy of recovery from others by surrounding himself with recovery without following the program. He will tell you, every day is a struggle to not let his irrational beliefs sabotage his recovery. Some days he is miserable, but what keeps him from relapsing is how much better his life has been and his relationship with his kids since he decided to sober up.

Obtaining sobriety is the beginning. Maintaining it is an ongoing, one-day-at-a-time exercise. But growth and knowledge of your new way of life is a forever learning experience. The more you improve your relationship with your creator, the more he will open your mind to learn and experience the many blessings that living a righteous life has to offer. When you utilize your mind to the fullest and open your eyes and ears, you will learn something new every day. Now, whether what you learn is constructive or destructive is determined by what you are seeking.

I try to meditate for at least half an hour a day. When I do, I spend ten minutes reflecting and twenty minutes conversing with my creator. I am a firm believer that everyone's relationship with their creator is different. My maker understands me and respects my cons just as much as my pros. He knows I'm not perfect. But he also knows I am not a prisoner of ignorance. Therefore, I know right from wrong. When I indulge in positivity, he blesses me with positive results. However, when I try to take shortcuts and do negative deeds, the punishment I receive is three times worse than the ones that are ignorant and don't know any better.

When I talk to my creator, I curse. Sometimes I get in my feelings. I ask him why he puts me through so much pain just to teach me a lesson. Why is it that a piece of shit type of person can do dirt and get away with it, but when I try to slip and slide through life, he knocks me to the ground? He always tends to answer me through experiences. He shows me day in and day out what he expects of me and why he put me on this earth. When I finally opened my eyes, I've come to the acceptance that I'm supposed to be on the side of good, not evil. I was meant to be a catalyst for the ones like me who came out of a system that was designed for us to lose yet beat the odds. A natural-born leader. Many catalysts have come before me and have lost their lives for the purpose of silencing them, preventing them from reaching the height of their true calling. My creator has given me visions of where my life will be in the next ten years if I just embrace his calling. I gracefully accept the duty and ask him to bless me with his will and the power to carry it out.

My maker loves to use divine interventions to both save me and teach me a lesson. He purposely takes me out of situations. For example, every time I go to jail, I either lose someone who probably would've stayed alive if I had made the right choices, or somebody dies in a situation that most likely I would've been in.

Before I got a 90-month sentence for some straight bullshit, during that time, my boy caught 25 years for a drug bust, 3 of my boys got murdered, and I lost my parents. My parents were devastating, which was my lesson. He also saved me, however. I would've been part of that drug bust, or I probably would've been doing time for murder, or worse, could've been the fourth homicide… who knows.

My choice of women to fall in love with. He helped me to decipher love from lust by showing me who really cared about me and the ones that were just using me. I had this one woman whom I grew up with. Her cousin is one of my best friends. I always wanted her. Light-skinned, pretty eyes, nice body… straight beautiful. I finally get her in 2020 and fall in love with her. I thought I had found one. To top it off, her cooking was amazing. The only issue, she had a drinking problem like me, and when she got drunk, she did whatever she wanted to do… including other men! I would've never found out until one day my nephew told me she left a cookout with her ex. I found out the hard way. I had fallen in love with a creep. My creator had taught me a lesson… you can be beautiful on the outside, but a piece of shit on the inside, lol.

I also dealt with a prostitute. A good girl though, lol, just young and money-hungry. When I went to treatment, I couldn't take care of her anymore. When I was there, I convinced her to stop hoeing in exchange for being with me. But like Snoop said… you can't turn a hoe into a housewife, lol.

Lastly, he separated me from friends that were detrimental to my health and the safety of my life. I used to mingle with some stone-cold murdering motherfuckers. Straight throwing rocks at the penitentiary. He had gotten my ass from out of that situation; I was almost in too deep.

With all that being said, me and my creator have a unique relationship. When he rewards me, he rewards me with opening doors to opportunities and giving me a clean conscience to progress mentally, emotionally, and financially in life. However, when he punishes me for doing shit, I know I'm not supposed to be doing… it's devastating.

Recovery is always a working process. It's like doing exercise to get in shape. You work hard and eat healthily to get to how you wish to look physically. Once you get there, then you must maintain it. You don't have to work out as hard, but you still must eat healthily and exercise to maintain the physique. Or else if you don't, what happens? You fall off. Gaining your sobriety from a substance is a starting point. Maintenance is necessary to stay clean. But growth mentally and having a solid relationship with your creator is major. When you accept that you are powerless to alcohol, you're asking your creator to flush away the negative thoughts and memories in your mind that trigger you to abuse a substance. You are asking him to grant you the wisdom and power to change your way of thinking. So that you can come up with positive plans derived from positive thinking which leads to you working on a positive, successful life.

For the record, I am still a work in progress. I am far from being recovered. Being honest with myself, yeah, I'm sober right now, if I wanted to drink now, could I? Absolutely. I choose not to which is a great start. However, the temptations in prison are far less great than the temptations of the world. Me being in prison working on my recovery is equivalent to me being in a long-term in-patient treatment center. It's easy to say no in a structured setting. The real test is in the world, where all your triggers are waiting for you, ready to suck you back in.

When I was released from prison, although I had twelve months of sobriety, I didn't go to my first meeting expecting to be awarded a one-year chip because I was sober in prison. I started from scratch. And it's not because I was worried about people judging me, because I could care less about what people think. It was because of me, and my conscience. I'm human. I'm not going to act like just because I wrote a book about recovery, that makes me exempt from slipping. All I can do is work on me, my way of thinking, and my relationship with my creator, one day at a time. I'm a student, not a teacher. We are all students. Your creator is the one that gives the lesson. Of course, the longer you've been in recovery, the more wisdom and understanding you have of remaining sober. But that doesn't mean that there are no longer days when your urges don't bother you, or something happens, such as an argument with a family member or a loved one. Getting laid off from work, a death of someone close to you. Even friends just enjoying themselves having a few drinks because they don't have the same problem as you... or so they believe they don't. Everyone's situation is different. You might just want to slow down from drinking or learn how to drink socially. That's when you must honestly ask yourself if you are mentally capable of not abusing it. Me personally, I know there is no drinking casually for me. All of that telling myself "Just one or two drinks and that's it" shit is out the window for me. If I'm going to drink, I'm going to drink, and once I start, I go every day until something bad ends up happening.

By me admitting that I have no control over my alcoholism, I basically gave up my privilege to drink. The creator blessed us with the power to create our own destiny, make our own choices, and decide our own fate. In life, we write the script for our own movie. It's up to you to either be a hero, or a villain.

Chapter 16

Suicide n. 1a: Intentional killing of oneself. b. A person who commits suicide. 2. Self-destructive action or course.

I have to speak on this because it's a very serious matter. Fentanyl is being put in everything, and it's killing people more than any other hard drug. People are dying left and right. I lost my big brother and one of my O.G.s that I looked up to like a big brother to a fentanyl overdose. I'm still grieving as we speak, but my grief is carried with mixed feelings.

My thing is this: unless you are suicidal, why would you indulge in a drug that you know there's a big possibility you can instantly die from? They both used to love heroin. I used to beg my brother to stop because he no longer knew what he was putting up his nose anymore. I'm going to make a hypothesis and say that 90% of heroin is being cut with fentanyl. There is no such thing as pure dope anymore. Pills are being pressed with fentanyl in them. Cocaine is being cut with it. Fentanyl is being used in everything because it takes a little to make a lot.

The sad part of it is this: all of this is known. Addicts are aware of this, yet they still use it. In fact, they are so addicted to it, they don't want the drugs unless it has fentanyl in it. Every pill you can think of is being pressed: Adderall, Percocet, Xanax, and ecstasy, all being pressed to look like the actual pill, when it's just fentanyl.

Young girls are turning up dead from popping pills, just to go to parties. College students ending up dead, thinking that they are taking Adderall to stay up and finish assignments, not knowing they're really taking fentanyl. The shit is deadly, and it's too late to control. Narcan doesn't even work for fentanyl. You surviving a fentanyl overdose is the luck of the draw. My brother and my O.G.'s luck ran out.

Although they had a disease, I'm still mad at them. I will always love them and miss them unconditionally, but them niggas weren't dummies.

They were smart and old enough to know when it was time to face reality. That shit wasn't the same as the drugs they were using back in the day. So, to me, they committed suicide. My brother died two units away from me at Plymouth House of Corrections, a maximum-security jail, with no contact visits. So, how he was able to obtain the drugs, they are going to have to explain to a lawyer when I get straight. But to think, something as little as a couple grains of salt can kill you instantly.

To keep it short and to the point: if you are using fentanyl and popping pressed pills, you are suicidal. Get help, don't wait until your luck runs out.

Chapter 17

Step 12: Having had a spiritual awakening as the result of these steps, we tried to carry this message to alcoholics, and to practice these principles in all our affairs.

In this step, which is the last but not the least, is where you realize that your step work never ends. The program is infinite. You learn from the steps, you live the steps, then you teach the steps.

Truthfully, me personally, I'm not at this level yet. Although my spirit has been awakened, I'm still in the process of not only living, but maintaining the work I've put in so far to utilize the steps in my everyday life. As humans, we learn better through trial and error. For me to say I'll never have to make amends again, would be a lie. But for me to say now, by having the power to embrace humility and accept the fact that I'm wrong, it gave me the ability to identify when and how promptly an amend should be made. Did I identify every characteristic whether good or bad by taking moral inventory of myself? Probably not. But did I gain the courage to do so? Whether it caused happiness or pain? Yes. It's called growth.

In the world of recovery, I'm still a grasshopper. Or better yet I'm still Daniel-san, or a young Luke Skywalker, gaining wisdom and understanding from the Miyagis and the Yodas of the world. The steps are guidelines to something far greater than just remaining sober. They help you through life, period. You don't have to be going through recovery from a substance. You can be recovering from the pain the world you came from has inflicted upon you, trying to regain peace within yourself and others.

Life recovery, I feel is more important than recovery from a substance. If you can recover from not making bad choices, doing bad deeds, trying to make short cuts to fortunes instead of working hard for it, and making excuses of why you can't change, the chances of you putting down an unwanted substance are far greater. Once again, you may think "I don't have an alcohol problem, what do I need to do my step work for?" Try this. By simply changing the word "alcohol" in the first step to whatever you honestly know you are powerless over, it will change the way you look at the steps. As a matter of fact, wherever the word "alcohol" is in the twelve steps, change it to your new accepted word.

It could be sex, money, greed, being a racist, or a sexist. You can even be powerless over food, or better yet, powerless, over having too much power. In the very next step, which is, came to believe that a power greater than ourselves could restore us to sanity, Allen Berger got me to understand the therapeutic value of that step: hope. Hope is an important ingredient to ALL forms of healing. With hope, resilience, and faith in your creator, we can be restored to sanity. But he won't guide you and help you if you're not willing to put the work in for yourself.

So, me being honest with myself, and you guys that took the time to hear me out. It's going to take some time for me to truly say I have completed the steps. Because before I can be completely comfortable with carrying out my message to other alcoholics, I want to master practicing the principles of the steps in all my affairs. You can know the steps and be able to recite them by heart. But to live them, breathe them, and embrace them is the difference between "Being" in recovery, and "living" in recovery. Most "Big Book thumpers" that are in recovery try so hard to be perfect, that they end up putting themselves under a microscope. Then when they unfortunately slip and everyone starts pointing fingers at them, they are too humiliated to bounce back. The ones that "live" in recovery, knows that although we work hard, and get upset if we slip, we are humans, and it's not the end of the world. Recovery is forever a working process. It's rare that you get it the first, second, or even the third time. Every slip is a learning experience, not a failure.

I now thank my creator for giving me the opportunity to find myself and re-evaluate my beliefs in this unfortunate circumstance. Learning how to accept and work on fixing my flaws, instead of running away from who I truly am. For also giving me the vision to see my true advantages, and utilizing them to uplift myself, and the people around me. When I leave this planet, I want to be remembered as an example of resilience. As a man who did his best to pull himself, and his people out of the mud of ignorance, to shower ourselves in the truth of our existence. I want to be a leader without the praise and recognizance of people who hold no true interest in the progress of people who grew up like me. Only interested in the exposure of our talents to contribute to their riches. I give credit to guys like Lebron James for knowing his true worth and not being willing to compromise it for nothing or no one. A true catalyst.

I will be the forefather of recovery when it's all said and done. I will say this to myself every day. I will speak it to existence. For the record, that doesn't mean I'm excluding white people (lol). I know white people who are just as urban as I am. But when I say urban, I mean that I'm representing the "Other side of America". The "Have-Nots". The ones who can't afford to go to places like Foundations in the Cape with the luxury of private chefs, eating prime rib for dinner. The ones who are battling not only addiction, but poverty, and mental health disorders stemming from having to figure out where to sleep, and how to eat every day. Or getting spat out of a correctional institution after doing many years for some bullshit and not being given any resources to help them re-enter and progress in society.

To make this possible, however, I must first work on myself. I can't be Robin Hood as long as I keep robbing the hood. I can't be constantly taking and never giving, unless I'm feeding poison to my people. I can't be a catalyst if I'm part of the problem that needs to be changed. The last step is for leaders who are sure of what they want to lead. Your purpose in life changes. It's not about you anymore. A real leader knows that the people he leads are valuable and they become more of a priority, even than himself. That's why your morals and your values must always stay intact. You are always depended on for answers and solutions to problems. How you solve these problems will always be praised or criticized. In the words of Napoleon Hill, "Leaders make choices, and rarely, if ever, change it."

Furthermore, I want to show my daughter that her father can do things the right way and still be successful. I want her to be proud that she's my daughter. I want to be able to change the perception in her brain about how I live my life. To do that, I must change the way I live—by not introducing her to females that are not worthy of the introduction. Honestly, I would hit the roof if my daughter ended up with someone like me. I would have no one to blame but myself. In order for me to change her belief that I'm an example of what a man is supposed to be, I first have to show her that I respect women.

I must embrace the steps and live them whether it's to remain in sobriety or to uphold my sanity. For me to feel comfortable to say I've completed these steps, I must carry out this new way of life in the world. I can preach all day but if I don't practice it, why speak of it? How can I teach something I can't show by example? Which has always been my problem with a therapist. You can't teach or counsel me about life when you've never experienced what it's like to be in my shoes. You can listen and opinionate, but you can't give me wisdom on something that I've lived through and you learned in a book.

I've had a taste of the life of sobriety. Falmouth, MA, was a life-changing and mind-altering experience. Every bit of me wants that life back. A life of no worries of the law, no worries of getting murdered, people looking at you with normalcy, peace, tranquility. However, I also know how it feels to lose all of it by making one bad choice. I know the feeling of humility and shame when you relapse and start to spiral downward. By working these steps and working on my belief system, I now know how to deal with it differently. Slipping is not a failure, it's a lesson. Depending on how, or if, you bounce back from it… determines if you make it a failure.

By living in fear of stepping to reality, you will never be able to honestly look at yourself and be happy with who you see. You will constantly run from the truth and be in denial of who you really are. Acceptance is the beginning of recovery... my name is James... in the Cape they call me Chocolate Jimmy... and I'm an alcoholic.

Who are you? Whoever it is... believe it... embrace it... accept it. I promise you, not only will you feel relieved of no longer hiding, life will be so much greater, and the pursuit of happiness will end up right at your door step... ONE LUV.

Final Thoughts

First and foremost, I would like to take this time to thank you for being a big part of my transition to recovery. While writing this book, it gave me the courage to face reality. I have a problem with alcohol, and with the help of my creator and the support of my peers, I can get through it one day at a time.

A lot of people in the world feel as though they don't have a problem, and in my opinion, they may not. Some people can control a substance and not let it control them. The problem comes when you know you can't control your addiction and you allow it to dictate your life. Once you realize that's the case, you realize you are therefore powerless and in need of help. Everyone doesn't need A.A. I will never look at someone differently because they drink, just because I can't control myself. I admire the fact that they are blessed to be able to drink socially and still function and have the discipline to live with or without it. To be honest, I feel that way about a person no matter what substance they indulge in. That is where people of the world go wrong. I had to learn how to change my belief on this topic as well. Casting judgment on people because they use a substance, not even knowing what type of person you're placing perceptions on.

Like for instance, how can I tell you that you have a problem, if you feel as though you don't have a problem? Especially when you are living a productive life, mentally, emotionally, and financially? Who am I to judge a man or women that has all their priorities in order? Who am I to diagnose you with a mental problem, when you believe you are perfectly normal? No one. Only you know when you have a problem. Only you have the power to come to that conclusion. Some people may think that that's not the right attitude to have, but to me it is. Because what's good for me, may not be good for you. Or vice versa. It's all about how we choose to live our lives.

The creator blessed us all to become our own unique person, with our own morals and principles. It's up to you to figure out what's a constructive or destructive decision. You have people in the world that love destruction. Although you, me, and the majority may look at them as being wrong, they may have their own reason to justify being right. The same goes with indulging in a substance. Whatever tickles your fancy, alcohol, opioids, narcotics, even marijuana, should not justify who you are to me as a person. You can be broke and like to drink and smoke weed and still be happier than a person sober with money.

I'm not ending this book on a confusing note, I'm just saying all of that to say this: just because I'm in recovery and I no longer indulge in shit I used to do in the past, I do not cast judgment on those that are not in recovery, or look at myself as being better than you, or smarter than you. All I know is that for me… alcohol in my life has done nothing but take away. I'm not successful at mixing alcohol with managing my priorities. I can't drink socially or responsibly. Therefore, I lost my privilege to drink. On the other hand, I commend the man or women that can control his or her life while indulging. I applaud you if you can still maintain your priorities and not allow a substance to dictate the outcome of your affairs. You CAN enjoy alcohol socially and responsibly.

I just want you to be honest with yourself if you know you have a problem. Don't live in denial. This book is a testimony for those who'd rather run and duck the truth than step to reality and face the fact that you have an uncontrollable and unmanageable beef with your choice of substance.

This book wasn't written solely for the purpose of recovering from substance abuse, either. It was also written to uplift those who are recovering from life—recovering from the bad choices they made, trying to get life back on track. The world doesn't end because of one bad choice, but your life can. Using the tools I've recited in this book from the resources I've used to help me re-evaluate my thought process helped me to identify my rights and my wrongs.

What you think is normally what you get. You think positive, you'll do positive. Negative thoughts come with negative outcomes and consequences. If people all around the world adopted this train of thought, just think how different society would be... picture that, lol. I am the guardian of my destiny. How I think and utilize the actions of my thoughts will determine the outcome of my life. So far, in my 40 years of being on this planet, it's safe to say that I've made more disastrous decisions than productive ones. Twelve and a half of them I spent in prison, wasting away. Years I can never get back but can take valuable lessons from. So, when the next time comes when I must make a "make or break" decision, I'll use my fucking brain.

It took a lot of bumps and bruises before I finally got the picture. I'm still licking my wounds. I had to fall all the way down for what I pray is for the last time, to enlighten myself and finally see what my creator was trying to show me for the last fifteen years, "James, you are living a lie, and it's time to face your true self or else, every time you don't listen, I am going to punch you in your face." I had to accept it, because now... I'm tired of black eyes.

I'm not Malcolm X, or Martin Luther King. I'm not Huey P. Newton, or Marcus Garvey. Nor do I want to be the next Obama. I'm simply James Dockery, an African American man that's a recovering alcoholic. And my journey, every trial and tribulation I've been through, contributes to my testimony. My testimony, I hope, will open the eyes of the young people. My story didn't start in Falmouth, or that day my probation officer called me. It started the moment I became conscious of my actions. It started the day I got my first ass-whooping from my mother. I want to catch the youth before they make that first bad, crucial decision or deter them from taking further ones. I figured, due to my popularity in my community, people will support my movement and furthermore motivate the youngsters to take the time to read some real shit, instead of watching hood movies and reading urban novels.

The story of Becky was for the purpose of showing you how caring and having a heart for people can bring you blessings in disguise and how money sometimes brings more problems than happiness. I dealt with her on a big brother level. I know that to help her I had to fully understand what she's battling. So, while I sat for a year, I wrote this book and I educated myself more vigorously on mental health disorders. I plan on taking substance abuse and mental health counseling classes to gain the knowledge to teach youngsters properly and to show that I have the credentials to do so.

I put my pride to the side, and I humbly made amends to the ones in my life whom I had hurt, affected in a negative way, or felt as though I had let down, including myself. I probably will never get over the fact that I wasn't there to properly lay my parents to rest. I still regret to this day some of the dumbass choices I've made in the past by trying to appease others and force myself to be someone I wasn't. The worst thing you can go through is feeling messed up you didn't get a chance to tell your sibling how you felt before he died. I had anger and resentment towards my brother before he passed. I love my brother, and it mentally messed me up to the point I was scared to experience how it felt being in this world without him. I had to tell him through this book, but not to his face, how he was my hero, my protector, and no matter right, wrong, or indifferent, my love for him is unconditional.

My daughter, I'm anxious to work on making a great future for her. So, when I leave this earth, I'll leave her and my grandson with something they will be proud of. Lastly, I had to suck it up and extend my hand to someone that I look at as a brother to me, with the hopes of him embracing it.

I had to break down the world of recovery to those who were unaware of the many fields of businesses that have their hands in the pockets of it. The pharmaceuticals, treatment facilities, the sober living game, all the ins and outs of why this big business needs people like me and you to relapse and be frequent members of the spin cycle. And like I said at the beginning of that chapter, a lot of people in the cult of A.A./N.A. are going to feel some type of way about me exposing the scheme and breaking it down the way I did because it's like being a traitor. I felt like Malcolm when he went to Mecca and found out the truth about Islam. This shit is all about a feeling of belonging to something. I used to look at Scott D like he was on to something; I learned he was. You know what though? When I had gotten released, I went back to the Cape and spent time with my recovery brothers. I might one day live there. Life was great. I'm chasing that feeling and I want it back.

Before I part ways with you let me leave you with some food for thought. Let's say if you were in the business of selling meat. Would you endorse being a vegan? Or, if you were the owner of Crisco oil, would you support air fryers? Hell no, you would figure out a way to keep people from becoming vegan, and you would support any movement against air fryers. That's how the big business of recovery feels about your sobriety. The only difference is they're like a wolf in sheep's clothing, acting like they care about reducing substance abuse, but at the same time cashing in off the spin cycle.

The R.E.T. technique, Rational Emotive Thinking, to control your thoughts. It works. You just must have the desire and the persistence to think what you want into existence. Think outside of the box, and figure it out, don't end up IN a box.

I am now brave enough to step up and face reality. And I have faith that one day, you will step to yours as well. PEACE.

References

"12 Stupid Things That Mess Up Recovery: Avoiding Relapse Through Self-Awareness and Right Action," written by Allen Berger, Ph.D.

"Rational Steps To Quitting Alcohol: When A.A. Doesn't Work For You," written by Albert Ellis, Ph.D., and Emmett Velten, Ph.D.

Some of my childhood friends

Me and my brother

Middle is my mother. left of her is my grandmother. To the right is my uncle johnny

Me & My daughter

James Dockery

My Grandson.

James Dockery.

My Niece

My daughter left side..my niece right side..my grandson in the middle

James Dockery

Marthan & her husband

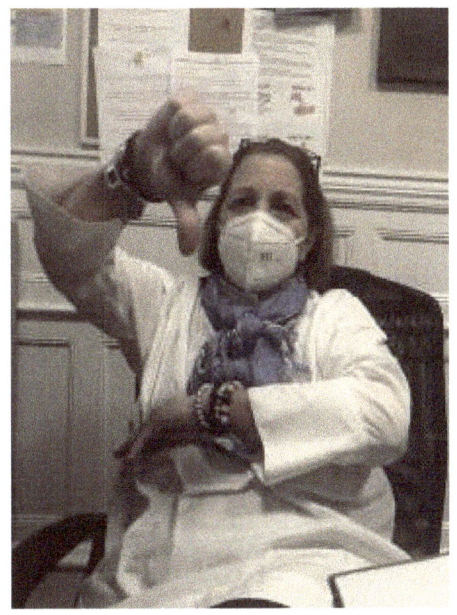

Marthan

Nick R.